Cassandra Design Patterns

Second Edition

Build industry-strength data storage solutions with
time-tested design methodologies using Cassandra

Rajanarayanan Thottuvaikkatumana

BIRMINGHAM - MUMBAI

Cassandra Design Patterns
Second Edition

First published: January 2014

Second edition: October 2015

Production reference: 1261015

Published by Packt Publishing Ltd.
Livery Place
35 Livery Street
Birmingham B3 2PB, UK.

ISBN 978-1-78528-570-7

www.packtpub.com

This book is an update to *Cassandra Design Patterns* by *Sanjay Sharma*.

Credits

Author
Rajanarayanan Thottuvaikkatumana

Reviewers
William Berg
Mark Kerzner
Alex Shvid

Commissioning Editor
Priya Singh

Acquisition Editor
Tushar Gupta

Content Development Editor
Samantha Gonsalves

Technical Editor
Anushree Arun Tendulkar

Copy Editor
Vatsal Surti

Project Coordinator
Kinjal Bari

Proofreader
Safis Editing

Indexer
Tejal Daruwale Soni

Production Coordinator
Aparna Bhagat

Cover Work
Aparna Bhagat

About the Author

Rajanarayanan Thottuvaikkatumana, "Raj", is a seasoned technologist with more than 23 years of software development experience at various multinational companies. He has lived and worked in India, Singapore, and the USA, and is presently based out of the UK. His experience includes architecting, designing, and developing software applications. He has worked on various technologies including major databases, application development platforms, web technologies, and big data technologies. Since 2000 onwards, he has been working mainly in Java-based technologies, and has been doing heavy-duty server-side programming in Java and Scala. He has worked on very highly concurrent, highly distributed, and high-transaction-volume systems with NoSQL data stores such as Cassandra and Riak and caching technologies such as Redis, Ehcache, and Chronicle Map. Raj has a lot of experience in integrating Cassandra with Spark and has shared the Scala code repository on GitHub.

Raj holds one master's degree in Mathematics and one master's degree in Computer Information Systems, and has many certifications in ITIL and Cloud Computing to his credit.

Apart from all this, Raj is a prolific corporate trainer on various technical subjects and has contributed to the Apache Cassandra project.

When not working with computers, Raj watches a lot of tennis and he is an avid listener of classical music.

Even though Raj has worked on many white papers and training materials, this is his first publication in the form of a book.

Acknowledgements

I would like to thank my father for showing me that there is no age barrier for embarking upon something totally new. I would like to thank my mother for showing me that relentless work will be fruitful one day. I would like to thank my wife for showing me that working towards perfection culminates in something beyond comparison. I would like to thank my teachers who have helped me to see learning as a continuous process. I would like to thank my geeky friends who collectively have solutions for almost any technical problem. Last but not the least, I would like to thank my present employer for gracefully giving me official permission to work on this project.

About the Reviewers

William Berg has been engineering software for the last several years, and has worked with Cassandra all that time. He works mainly with Java. He has also reviewed *Cassandra Design Patterns*, another *Packt Publishing* title. He also plays the bass guitar and produces electronic music.

Mark Kerzner holds degrees in law, math, and computer science. He is a software architect and has been working with Big Data for the last 7 years. He is a cofounder of Elephant Scale, a Big Data training and implementation company, and is the author of FreeEed, an open-source platform for eDiscovery based on Apache Hadoop. He has many authored books and patents to his credit. He loves learning languages, and is currently perfecting his Hebrew and Chinese.

> I would like to acknowledge the help of my colleagues, in particular Sujee Maniyam and, last but not least, of my multitalented family.

Alex Shvid is a Data Grid architect with more than 10 years of software experience in Fortune 500 companies with the focus on financial institutions. He has worked in the USA, Argentina, and Russia and has many architect and developer certifications, including those from Pivotal/Spring Source and Oracle. He is a regular speaker at user groups and conferences around the world such as the Java One and Cassandra meet ups. Alex works for PayPal in Silicon Valley, developing low-latency big data real-time solutions. His major specialization is in big data and fast data framework adoption for enterprise environments. He has participated in an open-source project Spring Data Cassandra module and developed a Dell Crowbar automation barclamp for Cassandra. Among his recent projects in Fast data are: integration of Gemfire from Pivotal as an event processing middleware solution and caching system for Gire (Buenos Aires, Argentina), Visa (Foster City, CA, USA), VMWare (Palo Alto, CA, USA) as well as the Coherence from Oracle for Analog (Boston, MA, USA), RCI (Parsippany, NJ, USA), and a custom data grid solution for Deutsche Bank (New York, NY, USA). When he is not working, Alex can usually be found hiking with his wife along the Coastal Trail in the San Francisco Bay Area

www.PacktPub.com

Support files, eBooks, discount offers, and more

For support files and downloads related to your book, please visit www.PacktPub.com.

Did you know that Packt offers eBook versions of every book published, with PDF and ePub files available? You can upgrade to the eBook version at www.PacktPub.com and as a print book customer, you are entitled to a discount on the eBook copy. Get in touch with us at service@packtpub.com for more details.

At www.PacktPub.com, you can also read a collection of free technical articles, sign up for a range of free newsletters and receive exclusive discounts and offers on Packt books and eBooks.

https://www2.packtpub.com/books/subscription/packtlib

Do you need instant solutions to your IT questions? PacktLib is Packt's online digital book library. Here, you can search, access, and read Packt's entire library of books.

Why subscribe?

- Fully searchable across every book published by Packt
- Copy and paste, print, and bookmark content
- On demand and accessible via a web browser

Free access for Packt account holders

If you have an account with Packt at www.PacktPub.com, you can use this to access PacktLib today and view 9 entirely free books. Simply use your login credentials for immediate access.

Table of Contents

Preface

Apache Cassandra is one of the most popular NoSQL data stores based on the research papers *Dynamo: Amazon's Highly Available Key-value Store* and *Bigtable: A Distributed Storage System for Structured Data*. Cassandra is implemented with the best features from both of these research papers. In general, NoSQL data stores can be classified into the following groups.

- Key-value data store
- Column-family data store
- Document data store
- Graph data store

Cassandra belongs to the column-family data store group. Cassandra's peer-to-peer architecture avoids single-point failures in the cluster of Cassandra nodes and gives the ability to distribute the nodes across racks or data centers. This makes Cassandra a linearly scalable data store. In other words, the greater your processing need, the more Cassandra nodes you can add to your cluster. Cassandra's multidata center support makes it a perfect choice to replicate data stores across data centers for disaster recovery, high availability, separating transaction processing, and analytical environments for building resiliency into the data store infrastructure.

The basic data abstraction in Cassandra starts with a column consisting of a name, value, timestamp, and optional time-to-live attributes. A row comes with a row key and a collection of sorted columns. A column family or a table is a collection of of rows. A keyspace is a collection of column families.

Cassandra 2.1 comes with a lot of new features making it an even more powerful data store than ever before. Now the new CQL keyword IF NOT EXISTS lets you check the existence of an object before Cassandra creates a new one. Lightweight transactions and the batching of CQL commands gives the user an ability to perform multistep atomic operations. Marking some columns in a column family as STATIC gives the user the ability to share data across all the rows of a given partition. The user-defined data type gives the power of modeling your data store very close to the real-world objects and objects used in the applications written using object-oriented programming languages. Collection indexes may be used to index and query collection data types in Cassandra. Row cache improvements, changes to reads and writes, off-heap memory tables, incremental node repair, and the new counter implementation all make Cassandra perform much better than its previous releases.

All the code samples that are used in this book are written for Cassandra 2.1.5. All the examples are as per the CQL specification 3.x. The pre-CQL Thrift API-based Cassandra CLI is being used to list the physical layout of the column families. An insight into the physical layout is very important because a wrong choice of a partition key or primary key will result in insidious performance problems. As a best practice, it is a good idea to create the column family, insert a couple of records, and use the list command in the Cassandra CLI with the column-family name. It will give the physical layout.

The term "design patterns" is a highly misinterpreted term in the software development community. In a very general sense, it is a set of solutions for some known problems in a very specific context. The way it is being used in this book is to describe a pattern of using certain features of Cassandra to solve some real-world problems. To refer to them and to identify them later, a name is also given to each of such design patterns. These pattern names may not be related at all to any similar sounding design pattern name used in other contexts and in other software development paradigms.

Users love Cassandra because of its SQL-like interface, CQL, and its features are very closely related to the RDBMS even though the paradigm is totally new. Application developers love Cassandra because of the plethora of drivers available in the market so that they can write applications in their preferred programming language. Architects love Cassandra because they can store structured, semi-structured, and unstructured data in it. Database administers love Cassandra because it comes with almost no maintenance overhead. Service managers love Cassandra because of the wonderful monitoring tools available in the market. CIOs love Cassandra because it gives value for their money. And, Cassandra works!

What this book covers

Chapter 1, *Co-existence Patterns*, discusses how Cassandra may be used in a legacy environment coexisting with RDBMSs.

Chapter 2, *RDBMS Migration Patterns*, discusses how some of the unique Cassandra features may be used to provide value and hence migrate traditional RDBMS data to Cassandra. It is a natural progression from coexistence with other legacy RDBMSs.

Chapter 3, *Cache Migration Patterns*, deals with some of the pitfalls of using caching solutions and how Cassandra may be used to overcome them.

Chapter 4, *CAP Patterns*, talks about data integrity considerations, consistency, availability, and partition tolerance and how some of the fine-tuning possibilities in Cassandra may be used to design powerful data stores.

Chapter 5, *Temporal Patterns*, discusses temporal data and how some of the features in Cassandra may be used to design powerful temporal data stores.

Chapter 6, *Analytics Patterns*, talks about the need for data analytics and how Cassandra in conjunction with Spark may be used to serve the data analysis use cases.

Chapter 7, *Designing Applications*, discusses designing a complete application that makes use of all the design patterns discussed in this book.

What you need for this book

Readers are advised to go through Cassandra data modeling before starting the journey of understanding *Cassandra Design Patterns, Second Edition*. An excellent book to start with data modeling is *Cassandra Data Modeling and Analysis*, C.Y. Kan, Packt Publishing. An understanding of RDBMS data modeling is a definite plus point.

This book has some version-specific content. The code examples refer to Cassandra Query Language (CQL). Cassandra 2.1.5 or above is the preferred version for references as well as for running the CQL code samples given in this book.

Who this book is for

This book is perfect for Cassandra developers who want to make use of the real power of Cassandra by taking their solutions to the next level. If you are an architect who is designing scalable Cassandra-based data solutions, this book is ideal for you to make use of the right Cassandra features in the right context to solve real-world problems. If you are already using Cassandra, this book will help you in leveraging its full potential.

Conventions

In this book, you will find a number of text styles that distinguish between different kinds of information. Here are some examples of these styles and an explanation of their meaning.

Code words in text, database table names, folder names, filenames, file extensions, pathnames, dummy URLs, user input, and Twitter handles are shown as follows: "In the `Order` table, `CustomerId` is a foreign key referring the `CustomerId` of the `Customer` table."

A block of code is set as follows:

```
CREATE KEYSPACE PacktCDP1 WITH replication = {'class':
'SimpleStrategy', 'replication_factor' : 3};
USE PacktCDP1;
CREATE TABLE CustomerOrder (
  CustomerId bigint,
  OrderId bigint,
  CustomerName text static,
  Email text static,
  OrderDate timestamp,
  OrderTotal float,
  PRIMARY KEY (CustomerId, OrderId)
  )
```

Any command-line input or output is written as follows:

```
USE PacktCDP1;
list CustomerOrder;
Using default limit of 100
Using default cell limit of 100
RowKey: 1
=> (name=1:, value=, timestamp=1433970886092681)
=> (name=1:customername, value=4d61726b2054686f6d6173,
timestamp=1433970886092681)
```

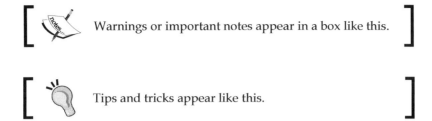

Warnings or important notes appear in a box like this.

Tips and tricks appear like this.

Reader feedback

Feedback from our readers is always welcome. Let us know what you think about this book—what you liked or disliked. Reader feedback is important for us as it helps us develop titles that you will really get the most out of.

To send us general feedback, simply e-mail feedback@packtpub.com, and mention the book's title in the subject of your message.

If there is a topic that you have expertise in and you are interested in either writing or contributing to a book, see our author guide at www.packtpub.com/authors.

Customer support

Now that you are the proud owner of a Packt book, we have a number of things to help you to get the most from your purchase.

Downloading the example code

You can download the example code files from your account at http://www.packtpub.com for all the Packt Publishing books you have purchased. If you purchased this book elsewhere, you can visit http://www.packtpub.com/support and register to have the files e-mailed directly to you.

Errata

Although we have taken every care to ensure the accuracy of our content, mistakes do happen. If you find a mistake in one of our books—maybe a mistake in the text or the code—we would be grateful if you could report this to us. By doing so, you can save other readers from frustration and help us improve subsequent versions of this book. If you find any errata, please report them by visiting `http://www.packtpub.com/submit-errata`, selecting your book, clicking on the Errata Submission Form link, and entering the details of your errata. Once your errata are verified, your submission will be accepted and the errata will be uploaded to our website or added to any list of existing errata under the Errata section of that title.

To view the previously submitted errata, go to `https://www.packtpub.com/books/content/support` and enter the name of the book in the search field. The required information will appear under the Errata section.

Piracy

Piracy of copyrighted material on the Internet is an ongoing problem across all media. At Packt, we take the protection of our copyright and licenses very seriously. If you come across any illegal copies of our works in any form on the Internet, please provide us with the location address or website name immediately so that we can pursue a remedy.

Please contact us at `copyright@packtpub.com` with a link to the suspected pirated material.

We appreciate your help in protecting our authors and our ability to bring you valuable content.

Questions

If you have a problem with any aspect of this book, you can contact us at `questions@packtpub.com`, and we will do our best to address the problem.

1
Co-existence Patterns

"It's coexistence or no existence"

– Bertrand Russell

Relational Database Management Systems (RDBMS) have been pervasive since the '70s. It is very difficult to find an organization without any RDBMS in their solution stack. Huge efforts have gone into the standardization of RDBMS. Because of that, if you are familiar with one RDBMS, switching over to another will not be a big problem. You will remain in the same paradigm without any major shifts. Pretty much all the RDBMS vendors offer a core set of features with standard interfaces and then include their own value-added features on top of it. There is a standardized language to interact with RDBMS called **Structured Query Language (SQL)**. The same queries written against one RDBMS will work without significant changes in another RDBMS. From a skill set perspective, this is a big advantage because you need not learn and relearn new dialects of these query languages as and when the products evolve. These enable the migration from one RDBMS to another RDBMS, which is a painless task. Many application designers designed the applications in an RDBMS agnostic way. In other words, the applications will work with multiple RDBMS. Just change some configuration file properties of the application, and it will start working with a different but supported RDBMS. Many software products are designed to support multiple RDBMS through their configuration file settings to suit the needs of the customers' preferred choice of RDBMS.

Mostly in RDBMS, a database schema organizes objects such as tables, views, indexes, stored procedures, sequences, and so on, into a logical group. Structured and related data is stored in tables as rows and columns. The primary key in a table uniquely identifies a row. There is a very strong theoretical background in the way data is stored in a table.

A table consists of rows and columns. Columns contain the fields, and rows contain the values of data. Rows are also called records or tuples. Tuple calculus, which was introduced by Edgar F. Codd as part of the relational model, serves as basis for the structured query language or SQL for this type of data model. Redundancy is avoided as much as possible. Wikipedia defines database normalization as follows:

> *"Database normalization is the process of organizing the attributes and tables of a relational database to minimize data redundancy."*

Since the emphasis is on avoiding redundancy, related data is spread across multiple tables, and they are joined together with SQL to present data in various application contexts. Multiple indexes that may be defined on various columns in a table can help data retrieval, sorting needs, and maintaining data integrity.

In the recent years, the amount of data that is being generated by various applications is really huge and the traditional RDBMS have started showing their age. Most of the RDBMS were not able to ingest various types of data into their schema. When the data starts flowing in quick succession, traditional RDBMS often become bottlenecks. When data is written into the RDBMS data stores in such speed, in a very short period of time, the need to add more nodes into the RDBMS cluster becomes necessary. The SQL performance degradation happens on distributed RDBMS. In other words, as we enter the era of big data, RDBMS could not handle the three Vs of data: Volume, Variety, and Velocity of data.

Many RDBMS vendors came up with solutions for handling the three Vs of data, but these came with a huge cost. The cost involved in the software licensing, the sophisticated hardware required for that, and the related eco-system of building a fault-tolerant solution stack, started affecting the bottom line in a big way. New generation Internet companies started thinking of different solutions to solve this problem, and very specialized data stores started coming up from these organizations and open source communities based on some of the popular research papers. These data stores are generally termed as NoSQL data stores, and they started addressing very specific data storage and retrieval needs. Cassandra is one of the highly successful NoSQL data stores, which has a very good similarity with traditional RDBMS. The advantage of this similarity comes in handy when Cassandra is adopted by an enterprise. The abstractions of a typical RDBMS and Cassandra have a few similarities. Because of this, new users can relate things to RDBMS and Cassandra. From a logical perspective Cassandra tables have a similarity with RDBMS-based tables in the view of the users, even though the underlying structures of these tables are totally different. Because of this, Cassandra is the best fit to be deployed along with the traditional RDBMS to solve some of the problems that RDBMS is not able to handle.

The caveat here is that because of the similarity of RDBMS tables and Cassandra column families (also known as Cassandra tables) in the view of the end users, many users and data modelers try to use Cassandra in exactly the same way as an RDBMS schema is being modeled, used, and is getting into the serious deployment issues. How do you prevent such pitfalls? At the outset, Cassandra may look like a traditional RDBMS data store. But the fact is that it is not the same. The key here is to understand the differences from a theoretical perspective as well as in a practical perspective, and follow the best practices prescribed by the creators of Cassandra.

 In Cassandra, the terms "column family" and "table" are synonymous. The **Cassandra Query Language** (**CQL**) command syntax uses the term "table."

Why can Cassandra be used along with other RDBMS? The answer to that lies in the limitations of RDBMS. Some of the obvious ones are cost savings, the need to scale out, handling high-volume traffic, complex queries slowing down response times, the data types are getting complex, and the list goes on and on. The most important aspect of the need for Cassandra to coexist with legacy RDBMS is that you need to preserve the investments made already and make sure that the current applications are working without any problems. So, you should protect your investments, make your future investments in a smart NoSQL store such as Cassandra, and follow the one-step-at-a-time approach.

A brief overview of Cassandra

Where do you start with Cassandra? The best place is to look at the new application development requirements and take it from there. Look at cases where there is a need to denormalize the RDBMS tables and keep all the data items together, which would have been distributed if you were to design the same solution in an RDBMS. If an application is writing a set of data items together into a data store, why do you want to separate them out? No need to worry about redundancy. This is the new NoSQL philosophy. This is the new way to look at data modeling in NoSQL data stores. Cassandra supports fast writes and reads. Initial versions of Cassandra had some performance problems, but a huge number of optimizations have gone into making the latest version of Cassandra perform much better for reads as well as writes. There is no problem with consuming space because the secondary storage is getting cheaper and cheaper. A word of caution here is that, it is fine to write the data into Cassandra, whatever the level of redundancy, but the data access use cases have to be thought through carefully before getting involved in the Cassandra data model. The data is stored in the disk, to be read at a later date. These reads have to be efficient, and it gives the required data in the desired sorted order.

In a nutshell, you should decide how do you want to store the data and make sure that it is giving you the data in the desired sort order. There is no hard and fast rule for this. It is purely up to the application requirements. That is, the other shift in the thought process.

Instead of thinking from the pure data model perspective, start thinking in terms of the application's perspective. How the data is generated by the application, what are the read requirements, what are the write requirements, what is the response time expected out of some of the use cases, and so on. Depending on these aspects, design the data model. In the big data world, the application becomes the first class citizen and the data model leaves the driving seat in the application design. Design the data model to serve the needs of the applications.

In any organization, new reporting requirements come all the time. The major challenge to generate reports is the underlying data store. In the RDBMS world, reporting is always a challenge. You may have to join multiple tables to generate even simple reports. Even though the RDBMS objects such as views, stored procedures, and indexes may be used to get the desired data for the reports, when the report is being generated, the query plan is going to be very complex most of the time. Consumption of the processing power is another need to consider when generating such reports on the fly. Because of these complexities, many times, for reporting requirements, it is common to keep separate tables containing data exported from the transactional tables. Martin Fowler emphasizes the need for separating reporting data from the operations data in his article, *Reporting Database*. He states:

> "*Most Enterprise Applications store persistent data with a database. This database supports operational updates of the application's state, and also various reports used for decision support and analysis. The operational needs and the reporting needs are, however, often quite different - with different requirements from a schema and different data access patterns. When this happens it's often a wise idea to separate the reporting needs into a reporting database, which takes a copy of the essential operational data but represents it in a different schema*".

This is a great opportunity to start with NoSQL stores such as Cassandra as a reporting data store.

Data aggregation and summarization are the common requirements in any organization. This helps to control data growth in by storing only the summary statistics and moving the transactional data into archives. Often, these aggregated and summarized data are used for statistical analysis. In many websites, you can see the summary of your data instantaneously when you log in to the site or when you perform transactions. Some of the examples include the available credit limit of credit cards, the available number of text messages, remaining international call minutes in a mobile phone account, and so on. Making the summary accurate and easily accessible is a big challenge. Most of the time, data aggregation and reporting go hand in hand. The aggregated data is used heavily in reports. The aggregation process speeds up the queries to a great extent. In RDBMS, it is always a challenge to aggregate data, and you can find new requirements coming all the time. This is another place you can start with NoSQL stores such as Cassandra.

Now, we are going to discuss some aspects of the denormalization, reporting, and aggregation of data using Cassandra as the preferred NoSQL data store.

Denormalization pattern

Denormalize the data and store them as column families in Cassandra. This is a very common practice in NoSQL data stores. There are many reasons why you might do this in Cassandra. The most important aspect is that Cassandra doesn't support joins between the column families. Redundancy is acceptable in Cassandra as storage is cheap, and this is more relevant for Cassandra because Cassandra runs on commodity hardware while many RDBMS systems need much better hardware specifications for the optimal performance when deployed in production environments. Moreover, the read and write operations are highly efficient even if the column families are huge in terms of the number of columns or rows. In the traditional RDBMS, you can create multiple indexes on a single table on various columns. But in Cassandra, secondary indexes are very costly and they affect the performance of reads and writes.

Motivations/solutions

In many situations, whenever a new requirement comes, if you think in the traditional RDBMS way, it will lead to many problems such as poor performance on read/write, long running processes, queries becoming overly complex, and so on. In this situation, one of the best approaches is to apply denormalization principles and design column families in Cassandra.

In the traditional RDBMS, the operational tables contain the data related to the current state of the entities and objects involved. So, maintaining lookups for preserving the integrity of the data is perfectly sensible. But when you have to maintain history, the concept of lookups will not work. For example, when you are generating a monthly bank account statement, the current statement should reflect the current address of the account holder. After the statement is generated, if the address of the account holder changes during the next reporting period, then the previous statements must not reflect the new address. They must have the old address, which was correct on the date that the statement was generated. In such situations, it does not make sense to keep a set of normalized tables for the historical data. The best thing to do at that time is to denormalize the data and maintain them in separate column families in Cassandra.

Complex queries are part of any system. In the RDBMS world, to shield the complexities of the query from the end users who design data entry forms, generate reports, typically views or stored procedures are designed. They are useful to run ad hoc queries, retrieve special set of records, and so on. Even though you solved the complexity problem from an end user perspective, the real problem remains unsolved. This means that when you run those queries or stored procedures, the complex joins of the tables are happening under the hood and on the fly. Because of this, the running time is greater and the processing requirements are huge. In the NoSQL world, it is better to denormalize the data and maintain them as big column families in Cassandra.

Immutable transactions are good candidates for denormalization because they capture the present state, the references it makes to other table records can be carried with the record of the transaction even if those references change in the future. The only use those transactions will have in the future is for read use cases. An immutable transaction means that once a transaction record it is written to the system, nothing is going to change in the future. There are many examples in real life that conform to this type, such as banking transaction records, weather station reading records, utility monitoring reading records, system monitoring records, service monitoring records, and you can find countless examples in your real-life applications. Event records originating from event management systems are possible candidates for denormalization, but caution has to be exercised when the event status changes and if the same record is being updated. If the event management systems generate multiple event records for state changes of the same event, denormalization will be a good fit. Capture these denormalized records in Cassandra.

Performance boosting requirements are good situations where denormalization may be applied. There may be many applications performing poorly when data is being written to the RDBMS. There is a strong possibility that this is happening because of the single transaction writing data into multiple tables and many indexes are being used in those tables. Careful analysis and proper characterization of the performance problems lead to data spread across multiple tables as the root cause many times. In such cases, denormalization of the data is the obvious option, and Cassandra comes as a good fit there.

Data modeling experts in the RDBMS world are typically not comfortable in denormalization because there is a general belief that the data integrity is maintained by the RDBMS table design itself, along with other features of RDBMS such as triggers, stored procedures, and so on. The data modeling in Cassandra is different. Here, along with the data model, all the application use cases where there is a data manipulation involved is also taken into consideration. So, the data integrity maintenance is the responsibility of the applications as well. Here, denormalization is the norm and the applications using the column families are supposed to handle the data integrity to make sure that the data is good.

Best practices

Denormalization must be done with utmost care. Normalization avoids redundancy and it promotes principles to maintain data integrity. When you denormalize, the only rule that is relaxed is redundancy. Data integrity must be maintained for a successful application, even if data is denormalized. With normalized tables in the RDBMS, the primary key constraints, foreign key constraints, unique key constraints and so on serve as watchdogs that maintain the data integrity even if the applications don't care about them. Verification and validation happens even at the RDBMS level. When moving to a NoSQL store such as Cassandra, many such goodies of RDBMS are lost. So, it is the responsibility of the application designers to prevent insert anomalies, update anomalies, and delete anomalies. Even though Cassandra comes with lightweight transactions, most of the data integrity control measures have to be taken from the application's side. Cassandra security has to be used heavily to make sure that only the proper applications with the right credentials are writing data to the column families.

Example

Let's take the case of a very simple normalized relation from the RDBMS world, as shown in the following screenshot. There are two tables in the relationship. One stores the customer details and the other stores the order details of the customers. This is a one-to-many relation where every customer record in the `Customer` table may have zero or more order records in the `Order` table. These two tables are joined by the primary `CustomerId` key.

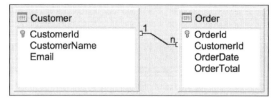

Figure 1

In the `Order` table, `CustomerId` is a foreign key referring the `CustomerId` of the `Customer` table. When you denormalize this to a Cassandra column family, it will look like the one given in the following figure. In Cassandra, the primary key is a combination of `CustomerId` and `OrderId` in the `CustomerOrder` column family. The `CustomerId` column becomes the partition key for this column family.

Figure 2

The denormalized Cassandra column family has all the fields of its normalized counter part. The following script can be used to create the column family in Cassandra. The following is the sequence of activities given in the script:

1. Create the key space.
2. Create the column family.
3. Insert one record into the column family.

The reason one record is inserted into the column family is to demonstrate the difference between the physical layout of the rows stored in Cassandra and how the queries are returning the same records.

It is very important to make sure that the physical layout of the column family is as expected and see how the columns are getting stored. To view the physical layout of the records, the old Cassandra CLI [cassandra-cli] must be used. This Cassandra CLI is used throughout this book in the context where there is a need to view the physical layout of the data in the column families.

Whenever a new column family is defined in Cassandra, it is very important to have an understanding of the physical and the logical views, and this helps the characterization of the column family growth and other behaviors. The following script is to be executed in cqlsh:

```
CREATE KEYSPACE PacktCDP1 WITH replication = {'class':
'SimpleStrategy', 'replication_factor' : 3};
USE PacktCDP1;
CREATE TABLE CustomerOrder (
  CustomerId bigint,
  OrderId bigint,
  CustomerName text static,
  Email text static,
  OrderDate timestamp,
  OrderTotal float,
  PRIMARY KEY (CustomerId, OrderId)
  )
  WITH CLUSTERING ORDER BY (OrderId DESC);

INSERT INTO CustomerOrder (CustomerId, OrderId, CustomerName, Email,
OrderDate, OrderTotal) VALUES (1,1,'Mark Thomas', 'mt@example.com',
1433970556, 112.50);
```

A great detail of attention needs to be given while choosing your primary key for a given column family. Conceptually, this is totally different from the RDBMS world. It is true that a primary key uniquely identifies a row. It may be an individual column or a combination of multiple columns. The differentiation comes in Cassandra is the way in which a row is stored in the physical nodes of Cassandra. The first column of the primary key combination is known as the partition key. All the rows in a given column family with the same partition key get stored in the same physical Cassandra node. The commands in the script here are to be executed in the Cassandra CLI interface:

```
USE PacktCDP1;

list CustomerOrder;

Using default limit of 100

Using default cell limit of 100
```

```
RowKey: 1
=> (name=1:, value=, timestamp=1433970886092681)
=> (name=1:customername, value=4d61726b2054686f6d6173,
timestamp=1433970886092681)
=> (name=1:email, value=6d74406578616d706c652e636f6d,
timestamp=1433970886092681)
=> (name=1:orderdate, value=000000005578a77c, timestamp=1433970886092681)
=> (name=1:ordertotal, value=42e10000, timestamp=1433970886092681)


1 Row Returned.
```

In the output, take a look at the row key. In the preceding example, as per the primary key used, the CustomerId field will be the row key. In other words, for every CustomerId, there will be one wide row. It is termed wide because all the records of a given CustomerId field, which is a partition key, will be stored in one row. One physical row of the Cassandra column family stores contains many records. In the use cases for which the column family is designed, it is important to make sure that if the row is growing, whether it is going to run out of the prescribed number of columns? If yes, then the design has to be looked at again and an appropriate partition key has to be identified. At the same time, it is not economical to have column families having only a very few rows and very few columns.

In a typical RDBMS table, the customer details will be in one or more tables. The transaction records such as order details will be in another table. But, here denormalization is applied, and data coming from those two logical entities are captured in one Cassandra column family.

The following CQL SELECT command gives the output in a human readable format:

```
SELECT * FROM CustomerOrder;
```

The output can be seen in this screenshot:

customerid	orderid	customername	email	orderdate	ordertotal
1	1	Mark Thomas	mt@example.com	1970-01-17 15:19:30+0000	112.5

Figure 3

Reporting pattern

Design separate column families in Cassandra for the reporting needs. Keep the operational data in RDBMS and the reporting data in Cassandra column families. The most important reason why this separation of concerns is good practice is because of the tunable consistency feature in Cassandra. Depending on the use cases and for performance reasons, various consistency parameters may be used in the Cassandra column families and in the applications using Cassandra for read and write operations. When data ingestion happens in Cassandra, the consistency parameters have to be tuned to have fast writes.

The consistency parameters used for fast writes may not be suitable for fast reads. So, it is better to design separate column families for reporting purposes. From the same operational data, if various types of reports have to be created, it may be wise to create separate column families for these different reporting requirements. It is also a common practice to preprocess the operational data to generate fast reports. Historical reporting, data archival, statistical analysis, providing data feeds, inputs for machine learning algorithms such as recommendation systems and so on benefit a lot from accessing data from the Cassandra column families specifically designed for reporting.

Motivations/solutions

Coming from the RDBMS world, people rarely think about the reporting needs in the very beginning. The main reason behind that is, there is good flexibility with the SQL queries, and you can pretty much get any kind of report from the RDBMS tables because you may join RDBMS tables. So, the application designers and data modelers focused on the data and the business logic first. Then, they came to thinking about the reports. Even though this strategy worked, it introduced lots of application performance problems either toward the end of the application development or when the data volume has grown beyond certain limit. The best thing to do in these kind of situations is to design separate Cassandra column families for the reporting needs.

In social media and real media applications commonly used by millions of users at a given time, reporting needs are huge. Most importantly, the performance of those reports are even more paramount. For example, in a movie streaming website, users post videos. Users follow other users. The followers like the videos posted by the users whom they are following. Now, take the two important views in the website: the first one that gives the list of videos liked by a given user, the second one gives the list of users liking a given video. In the RDBMS world, it is fine to use one table to store the data items to generate these two reports. In Cassandra, it is better to define two column families to generate these two reports. You may be wondering why this can't be achieved by reading out of a single column family. The reason is that the sorting order matters in Cassandra, and the records are stored in sorted order.

In Cassandra, it may be necessary to create different column families to produce different reports. As mentioned earlier, it is fine to write the same piece of data into multiple Cassandra column families. There is no need to panic as the latest versions of Cassandra comes with batching capability for data manipulation operations. In this way, the data integrity may be ensured. It may not be as flexible and powerful as many RDBMS, but there are ways to do this in Cassandra. For example, take the case of a hypothetical Twitter-like application.

Users tweet and the tweets have to be shown differently in the default view, differently in the listing using hashtags, differently in the user time line, and so on. Assuming that Cassandra is being used for storing the tweets, you may design different Cassandra column families for materializing these different views. When a new tweet comes in, that record will be inserted into all these different column families. To maintain the data integrity, all these INSERT statements may be designed as atomic unit of statements by enclosing them between the BEGIN BATCH and APPLY BATCH statements of CQL, as batches are atomic by default.

When it comes to reporting, RDBMS fails miserably in many use cases. This is seen when the report data is produced by many table joins, and the number of records in these tables are huge. This is a common situation when there is complex business logic to be applied to the operational data stored in the RDBMS before producing the reports. In such situations, it is always better to go with creating separate column families in Cassandra for the reporting needs. This may be done in two ways. The first method is the online way, in which the operational data is transformed into analytical or reporting data and stored in Cassandra column families. The second method is the batching way. In regular intervals, transform the operational data into analytical or reporting data in a batch process with business logic processors storing the data in Cassandra column families.

Predictive analytics or predictive modeling is very common these days in the commercial and scientific applications. A huge amount of operational data is processed, sliced, and diced by the data scientists using various machine learning algorithms and produces outputs for solving classification, regression, and clustering problems. These are highly calculation-intensive operations and deals with huge amount of operational data. It is practically impossible to do these calculations on the fly for the instantaneous requests from the users of the system. In this situation, the best course of action is to continually process the data and store the outputs in Cassandra column families.

> There is a huge difference between the reporting data and analytical data. The former deals with producing the data from the data store as per the user's selection criteria. The latter deals with the data to be processed to give a result to the user as an answer to some of their questions, such as "why there is a budget overrun this year?", "when the forecast and the actual started deviating?" and so on. Whenever such questions are asked, the analytical data is processed and a result is given.

Graphical representation of vital statistics is an important use case in many of the applications. These days many applications provide huge amount of customization for the users to generate user-defined graphs and charts. For making this happen, there are sophisticated graphing and charting software packages that are available in the market. Many of these software packages expect the data in certain format to produce the graphical images. Most of the time, the operational data may not be available in the specific format suitable for these specialized software packages. In these situations, the best choice of any application designer is to transform the operational data to suit the graphing and charting requirements. This is a good opportunity to use separate Cassandra column families to store the data specific for the graphing and charting.

Operational and historical reporting are two different types of needs in many applications. Operational data is used to report the present, and historical data is used to report the past. Even in the operational reporting use cases, there are very good reasons to separate the reporting data to different Cassandra column families. In the historical reporting use cases, it is even more important because the data grows over a period of time. If the velocity of the operational data is very high, then the historical reporting becomes even more cumbersome. Bank account statements, credit card statements, payslips, telephone bills, and so on, are very good examples of historical reporting use cases.

In the past, organizations used to keep the historical data as long as it is needed in the system for the compliance and governance requirements. Things have changed. Many organizations have started keeping the data eternally to provide value-added services as the storage is becoming cheaper and cheaper these days. Cassandra is a linearly scalable NoSQL data store. The more storage requirements you have, the more nodes you can add to its cluster as and when you need without any need to reconfigure or any downtime, and the cluster will start making use of the newly added nodes. Read operations are really fast, so reporting is a highly used use case supported by Cassandra column families with the clever use of tunable consistency.

In the old generation applications, operational data is archived for posterity and auditing purposes. Typically, after its decided lifetime, operational data is taken offline and archived so that the data growth is not affecting the day-to-day operations of the system. The main reason why this archival is needed is because of the constraints in the data storage solutions and the RDBMS used. Clustering and scaling out of RDBMS-based data store is very difficult and extremely expensive. The new generation NoSQL data stores such as Cassandra are designed to scale out and run on commodity hardware. So, the need to take the data offline doesn't exist at all. Design Cassandra column families to hold the data marked for archival and they can be kept online for ever. Watch out the data growth and keep on adding more and more Cassandra nodes into the Cassandra cluster as and when required.

The emergence of cloud as the platform of choice and proliferation of **Software as a Service (SaaS)** applications introduced one more complexity into the application design, which is multitenancy. Multitenancy promotes the use of one instance of an application catering to the needs of multiple customers. Most of these SaaS applications give its customers a good amount of customization in terms of the features and reports. The service providers who host these SaaS have a new challenge of maintaining customer specific data and reports. This is a good use case where separate Cassandra column families to be used for maintaining customer-specific data needed for the tailor made reports.

Financial exchanges, trading systems, mobile phone services, weather forecasting systems, airline reservation systems, and the like produce high-volume data and process them with subsecond response to their end users. Obviously, the reporting needs are also huge in those applications in terms of the number of records to be processed and the complexity of data processing required. In all these systems-separating operations data and reporting data is a very important requirement. Cassandra is a good fit in all these reporting use cases.

Data transformation is an important step in producing many reports. In the enterprise application integration use cases, often one application will have to provide data to another application in a certain format. XML and JSON are two important data exchange formats. In applications with service-oriented architecture, whether they consume or produce services, data is required in specific formats. Whatever the technology used to perform the transformation may be, because of the volume of the data, it is practically impossible to process these data as and when required on a real-time basis. Preprocessing is required in many situations to produce the data in specific formats. Even though RDBMS supports data types such as BLOB and CLOB to store huge chunk of data, often the limitations of RDBMS will take effect. NoSQL data stores such as Cassandra are designed to handle very sophisticated data types built using user-defined data types, and it is easy to use them for storing the preprocessed data for the future reporting purposes.

Providing data feeds to external systems is a very common requirement these days. This is a very effective mechanism for disseminating data asynchronously to the subscribers of the data through popular mechanisms such as RSS feeds. The data designated for the data feeds must be derived from the operational data. Cassandra column families may be designed to serve such requirements.

Best practices

Separation of operational and reporting data stores is a good idea in many cases, but care must be taken to check if it is violating any of the data integrity or business logic invariants in the system. Immutable data items are really good candidates for this separation because they are not going to be changed anytime in the future. It is better to keep the frequently changing data items in the operational data stores itself. In Cassandra, if column families are used only for reporting purposes, care must be taken on how to load the data into the column families. Typically, these column families will be optimized for fast reads. If too many writes into those column families are going to take place, the consistency parameters will have to be tuned very well so that it does not defeat the original purpose of creating those column families, which is to read data from it. It is very difficult to tune Cassandra column families to suit the needs of very fast writes and reads. One of these will need to be compromised. Since the original purpose of these column families is to provide fast reads, the speed of writes must be controlled. More detailed treatment on the tuning for fast reads and fast writes in Cassandra column families is given in the coming chapters of this book.

Example

Let's take the case of a normalized set of tables from an application using RDBMS, as shown in *Figure 4*. There are three tables in the relation. One stores the customer details, another one stores the order details, and the third one stores the order-line items. Assume that this is an operational table and the data size is huge. There is a one-to-many relation between the Customer table and the Order table. For every customer record in the Customer table, there may be zero or more order records in the Order table. There is a one-to-many relation between the Order table and the OrderItems table. For every order record in the Order table, there may be zero or more order item records in the OrderItems table.

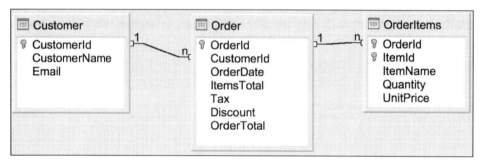

Figure 4

Assume that the requirement is to create a Cassandra column family to generate a monthly customer order summary report. The report should contain one record for each customer containing the order total for that month. The Cassandra column family will look like the one given in the *Figure 5*.

In the Cassandra column family MonthlyCustomerOrder, a combination of CustomerId, OrderYear, and OrderMonth columns form the primary key. The CustomerId column will be the partition key. In other words, all the records for a given customer will be stored in one wide row of the column family.

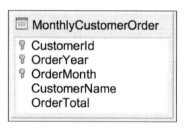

Figure 5

Assuming that the key space is created using the scripts given *Figure 3*, the scripts given here will create only the required column family and then in: record. Filling in the data in this column family may be done on a real-tim as a batch process. Since the data required for filling the Cassandra colum is not readily available from the RDBMS tables, a preprocessing needs to to prepare the data that goes into this Cassandra column family:

```
USE PacktCDP1;
CREATE TABLE MonthlyCustomerOrder (
  CustomerId bigint,
  OrderYear int,
  OrderMonth int,
  CustomerName text static,
  OrderTotal float,
  PRIMARY KEY (CustomerId, OrderYear, OrderMonth)
  )
  WITH CLUSTERING ORDER BY (OrderYear DESC, OrderMonth DESC);

  INSERT INTO MonthlyCustomerOrder (CustomerId, OrderYear, OrderMonth,
  CustomerName, OrderTotal) VALUES (1,2015,6,'George Thomas', 255.5);
```

The following script gives the details of how the row in the Cassandra column family is physically stored. The commands given here are to be executed in the Cassandra CLI interface:

```
USE PacktCDP1;

list MonthlyCustomerOrder;

Using default limit of 100

Using default cell limit of 100

RowKey: 1

=> (name=2015:6:, value=, timestamp=1434231618305061)

=> (name=2015:6:customername, value=476f657267652054686f6d6173,
timestamp=1434231618305061)

=> (name=2015:6:ordertotal, value=437f8000, timestamp=1434231618305061)


1 Row Returned.

Elapsed time: 42 msec(s).
```

The CQL SELECT command given in *Figure 6* gives the output in a human readable format:

```
SELECT * FROM MonthlyCustomerOrder;
```

```
 customerid | orderyear | ordermonth | customername  | ordertotal
------------+-----------+------------+---------------+------------
          1 |      2015 |          6 | Goerge Thomas |      255.5
```

Figure 6

Aggregation pattern

Design separate Cassandra column families to store the aggregated and summarized operational data. Aggregated data is used for various reporting and analytical purposes. Cassandra does not inherently support any joins between column families. Cassandra does not support the commonly seen SQL aggregation constructs such as GROUP BY, HAVING, and so on. Because of these constraints, it is better to preprocess the operational data to do the aggregation, summarization, and storage of the processed data in Cassandra column families. The lack of ability to do real-time aggregation using CQL can be converted to an advantage of using Cassandra, which is serving fast reads of already aggregated data and exploiting its highly scalable architecture.

Motivations/solutions

SQL on RDBMS provides a great deal of flexibility to store and retrieve data, apply computations, perform aggregations, and summarizations effortlessly. All these work fine as long as the data volume is manageable. The moment the data volume goes above the threshold and there is need to scale out to a distributed model, everything comes to a screeching halt. When the data is distributed across multiple RDBMS hosts, the queries and computations on top of it crawl even more. Because of these limitations, the separation of aggregated and operational data into separate tables became common practice. In this era of **Internet of Things (IoT)**, even aggregated and summarized data starts overflowing within no time. In such situations, it is a good idea to move these already processed, aggregated, and summarized data into Cassandra column families. Cassandra can handle loads of such data and provide ultra-fast reads, even when the nodes are highly distributed across multiple racks and data centers.

Over a period of a couple of decades, there has been a clear change in the trend of how the data is aggregated. Originally, the RDBMS table data was processed through batch application processes, and the data was aggregated. Then, the traditional batch processes gave way to the divide-and-conquer methodologies such as Map/Reduce and Hadoop, to aggregate the data, but even then the aggregated data remained in separate RDBMS instances or in some distributed filesystems such as **Hadoop Distributed File System (HDFS)**. The HDFS filesystem-based storage was good in some use cases, but the data access and reporting became difficult as the big data market was maturing in terms of the available tools and applications. Now, NoSQL data stores such as Cassandra offer good interoperability with other applications, and they can be used as a highly scalable data storage solution.

The drill-down capability has been a very common feature in many of the applications for a long time. In the user interfaces, a very high level aggregated and summarized data in the form of tables or graphs are presented. When the user clicks on a link, button, or section on the graph, the application presents the associated data that was used to create the aggregation or summarization. Typically, there will be multiple levels of these drill-downs and for providing that, the data must be aggregated at different levels. All of these operations are very computationally intensive, as well as expensive. Cassandra is a good fit to store these preprocessed data coming from the RDBMS tables. There are many data processing applications that make use of the multicore architecture of the modern computers and do the tasks asynchronously. Even though the RDBMS perform well when scaled up by making use of the multiple processing cores and huge memory seen in modern hardware, as mentioned earlier, the RDBMS don't perform well when it is scaled out especially where there are multiple table joins. Proper use of these data processing tools in conjunction with Cassandra will provide great value in storing the aggregated and summarized data.

Many organizations sell the data generated from their applications. Depending on the sensitivity of the data and the potential dangers of violating data protection and privacy laws, data aggregation becomes a mandatory requirement. Often, these aggregated data-for-sale need to be completely separated from the organization's live data. This data goes with totally different access controls, even at the level of hosting location. Cassandra is a good fit for this use case.

Marketing analytics use lots of aggregation. For example, in the case of retail transactions happening in a store, a third-party marketing analytics organization will not be given the individual transaction records. Instead, the transaction data is aggregated and it is ensured that all the personally identifiable data is masked or removed before being handed over for any analytical purposes. Consolidation, aggregation, and summarization are common needs here. Many organizations gather data from various marketing channels of the same organization itself to generate a common view of the marketing efforts. Many organizations find new avenues of creating new applications and value added services based out of these aggregated data. When new initiatives such as these come, separation of concerns plays an important role here and often business incubation teams or research and development units take these initiatives to the next level. These are the times the teams really think out of the box and start using new technologies. They completely move away from the legacy technologies to exploit the economies of scale. Exploration of new technologies happens when the legacy technologies have pain points, and when there is a need to reduce cost incurred due to specialized hardware requirements along with software license costs. Exploration with new technologies also happens when there is a totally new requirement that cannot be served by the ecosystem in use. Cassandra is a good fit in these use cases because many Internet scale applications use Cassandra heavily for heavy-duty data storage requirements running on commodity hardware, thus providing value for money.

Data visualization products use a lot of aggregation. Many such products are plagued by using too much data. Clutter drives users away and the information is lost in the abundant usage of data. Seeing all these problems, many other products are using aggregated data to visualize and provide drill down or other similar techniques in the visualization. Cassandra can be used store multilevel aggregated data in its column families.

Data warehousing solutions are fast moving away from RDBMS to NoSQL such as Cassandra. Data warehousing projects deal with huge amount of data and does lots of aggregation and summarization. When it comes to huge amount of data, scaling out beyond a single server is a mandatory requirement. Cassandra fits very well there. Data warehousing solutions also need to support various data processing tools. There are many drivers available in the market to connect to Cassandra. Many data processing and analytics tools such as Apache Spark work very well with Cassandra.

Online shopping sites generate lots of sale records. Many of them are still using RDBMS as their preferred data stores. It is practically impossible to generate a report, including all these sales records. So even in the basic reporting itself, aggregation plays a big role. These aggregated data is used for sales forecasting, trending, and undergoing further processing. NoSQL data stores such as Cassandra become the preferred choice of many to store these aggregated data.

Proliferation of data products mandated the need to process the data in a totally new way with lots of transformations from one format to another. Aggregation and summarization has become part of all these processes. Here, even the traditional SQL-based RDBMS fail because the processing needs are beyond SQL's limited capabilities. The RDBMS fails here on two counts. The first one being the inability to process data, and the second one being the inability to store the processed data that comes in totally different formats. Even Cassandra fails on the first one, but it scores better on the second one because it can store very sophisticated data types and can scale out to the roof. A detailed coverage on the Cassandra data types is coming in the upcoming chapters of this book.

Best practices

When doing aggregation and storing the aggregated data in Cassandra, care must be taken in the drill-down use cases. The drill-down use cases uses both the operational and aggregated data as Cassandra is coexisting with the existing RDBMS. When the operational data is coming from traditional RDBMS tables and the aggregated data coming from the Cassandra data stores, there are good chances of tight coupling of application components. If a design is not done properly and not thoughtfully crafted, the application maintenance will be a nightmare.

The word **aggregation** is used in a totally different context in the NoSQL parlance. It is used to consolidate many related data items into one single unit and stored in the NoSQL data stores to store and retrieve as a single unit. Martin Fowler used this term in his article titled *Aggregate Oriented Database* and in that he uses the term aggregation in this way:

"Aggregates make natural units for distribution strategies such as sharding, since you have a large clump of data that you expect to be accessed together. An aggregate also makes a lot of sense to an application programmer. If you're capturing a screenful of information and storing it in a relational database, you have to decompose that information into rows before storing it away. An aggregate makes for a much simpler mapping - which is why many early adopters of NoSQL databases report that it's an easier programming model." When this type of aggregation is being used in Cassandra, care must be taken and don't store a big load of data items in as a blob.

The application logic must be carefully thought through in order to make sure that there is a proper sync-up between the operational and the aggregated data. If out of sync, this will become very obvious in the drill-down use cases because the aggregate record will show one value and the details will show a different value.

It is a good practice to store the data in Cassandra with proper structure always, even if the number of data items is large. It is comparatively easy to manage structured data than unstructured data.

Example

Let's take the case of a normalized set of tables from an application using RDBMS as shown in the *Figure 7*:

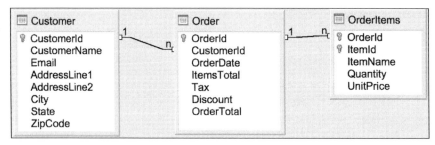

Figure 7

There are three tables in the relation. The first stores the customer details, the second one stores the order details, and the third one stores the order line items. Assume that this is an operational table and the data size is huge. There is a one-to-many relation between the Customer and Order table. For every customer record in the Customer table, there may be zero or more order records in the Order table. There is a one-to-many relation between the Order and OrderItems table. For every order record in the Order table, there may be zero or more order item records in the OrderItems table.

Assume that the requirement is to create an aggregation of the orders to have a monthly city order summary report. The Cassandra column family will look like the following screenshot:

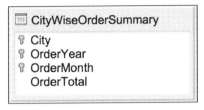

Figure 8

In the `CityWiseOrderSummary` column family, a combination of `City`, `OrderYear`, and `OrderMonth` form the primary key. The `City` column will be the partition key. In other words, all the order aggregate data related to a given city will be stored in a single wide row.

Assuming that the key space is created using the scripts given in the example of de-Normalization pattern, the scripts given here will create only the required column family and then insert a couple of records. Filling of the data in this column family may be done on a real-time basis or as a batch process. Since the data required for filling the Cassandra column family is not readily available from the RDBMS tables, a preprocessing needs to be done to prepare the data that goes into this Cassandra column family:

```
USE PacktCDP1;
CREATE TABLE CityWiseOrderSummary
(
  City text,
  OrderYear int,
  OrderMonth int,
  OrderTotal float,
  PRIMARY KEY (City, OrderYear, OrderMonth)
)
WITH CLUSTERING ORDER BY (OrderYear DESC, OrderMonth DESC);

INSERT INTO CityWiseOrderSummary (City, OrderYear, OrderMonth,
OrderTotal) VALUES ('Leeds',2015,6,8500);
INSERT INTO CityWiseOrderSummary (City, OrderYear, OrderMonth,
OrderTotal) VALUES ('London',2015,6,8500);
```

The following script gives the details of how the row in the Cassandra column family is physically stored. The commands given here are to be executed in the Cassandra CLI interface:

```
USE PacktCDP1;
list CityWiseOrderSummary;
Using default limit of 100
Using default cell limit of 100
RowKey: London
=> (name=2015:6:, value=, timestamp=1434313711537934)
=> (name=2015:6:ordertotal, value=4604d000, timestamp=1434313711537934)

RowKey: Leeds
=> (name=2015:6:, value=, timestamp=1434313683491588)
=> (name=2015:6:ordertotal, value=4604d000, timestamp=1434313683491588)

2 Rows Returned.
Elapsed time: 5.17 msec(s).
```

The SELECT command given in *Figure 9* gives the output in a human readable format:

```
SELECT * FROM CityWiseOrderSummary;
```

city	orderyear	ordermonth	ordertotal
London	2015	6	8500
Leeds	2015	6	8500

Figure 9

Just like the way the city-wise order summary is created, if we also need to create a state-wise order summary from the RDBMS tables given in *Figure 7*, a separate Cassandra column family will need to be created and the appropriate application processing needs to be done to fill in the data into that Cassandra column family.

References

The following links can be referred to for further information:

- `https://en.wikipedia.org/wiki/Database_normalization`
- `http://martinfowler.com/bliki/ReportingDatabase.html`
- `http://martinfowler.com/bliki/AggregateOrientedDatabase.html`

Summary

The coexistence of RDBMS and NoSQL data stores such as Cassandra is very much possible, feasible, and sensible; and this is the only way to get started with the NoSQL movement, unless you are embarking on a totally new product development from scratch. Here, only a few patterns have been discussed. But there are many other different ways in which Cassandra can harmoniously coexist with other genres of data stores. All the examples given in this chapter were based on hypothetical requirements just to demonstrate the design pattern. Those who actually implement the appropriate design patterns in their Cassandra data model may use it as a guidance to implement real-world solutions.

Coexistence of two or more technologies gives great confidence to the system architects as well as the end users. This opens a door to a great opportunity for the new technology to expand and flourish. Then, the next step that anybody would take is to migrate from the old technology to the new technology wherever it is applicable. There are some great use cases where the migration from RDBMS to Cassandra makes perfect sense. In the next chapter, we will discuss that further.

RDBMS Migration Patterns

2

"The secret of change is to focus all of your energy, not on fighting the old, but on building the new"

– Dan Millman

A big bang approach to any kind of technology migration is not advisable. A series of deliberations have to take place before the eventual and complete change over. Migration from RDBMS to Cassandra is no different. Any new technology replacing an old one must coexist harmoniously with the old technology, at least for a short period of time. This gives a lot of confidence in the new technology to the stakeholders.

Many technology pundits provide you with various approaches for the RDBMS to NoSQL migration strategies. Many such guidelines are specific to particular NoSQL data stores, paying attention to specific areas, and most of the time that will end up paying attention to the process rather than the technology. Here, the point of discussion is not the process of the migration. All the technical, economical, and logistical due diligence must happen for migration to Cassandra as well. However, these discussions are beyond the scope of this book.

The migration from RDBMS to Cassandra is not an easy task, mainly because the RDBMS-based systems are time-tested and trustworthy in most organizations. So, migrating from such a robust RDBMS-based system to Cassandra is not going to be easy.

The migration from RDBMS to Cassandra discussed here does not mean any one-to-one porting of the RDBMS data models to the Cassandra data models. The word "migration" used here is in a much wider sense. Nobody migrates from one paradigm to another without seeing any benefits. Here, greater emphasis is given to the benefits by making use of some of the new and unique features of Cassandra.

The first step for a successful migration from RDBMS to Cassandra has already been discussed in the preceding chapter—the coexistence of Cassandra with the RDBMS from where the migration is going to happen. Once the stakeholders are happy with the new technology, the migration begins. The case of Cassandra is no different. It can be made to coexist with any RDBMS.

The migration from RDBMS to Cassandra should bring some positive change in the technical solution stack of the organization. It should provide quick wins and show its valuable presence in the technological ecosystem where it is going to be used. One of the best approaches for achieving this goal is to exploit some of the new or unique features in Cassandra, which many of the traditional RDBMSs don't have. This also prevents Cassandra from being used like any other RDBMS. Cassandra is unique. Cassandra is not an RDBMS. The approach of banking on the unique features is not only applicable to the RDBMS to Cassandra migration, but also to any migration from one paradigm to another. Some of the design patterns that are going to be discussed in this chapter revolve around very simple and important features of Cassandra; however, they have profound application potential when designing the next generation NoSQL data stores using Cassandra. A wise usage of these unique features in Cassandra will give you a head start on the eventual complete migration from RDBMS.

Modeling a collection of objects in RDBMS is a real pain because multiple tables have to be defined and a join is required to access data. Many RDBMSs offer this by providing the capability to define user-defined data types, but there is no standardization at all in this space. Collection objects are very commonly seen in real-world applications. Lists of actions, tuples of related values, sets of objects, dictionaries, and other such things appear quite often in applications. Cassandra has very elegant ways to model these because they are data types in column families.

Counting is a very commonly required process in many business processes and applications. In an RDBMS, this has to be modeled in the form of integers or long numbers, but a lot of the time, applications make big mistakes by using them in the wrong ways. Cassandra has a counter data type in the column family that alleviates this problem.

Counters are used for counting things. The only logical operations that are to be performed in counters are increment and decrement—count up or count down. It is also possible to increase or decrease the counters by a given value. If a real-world object that is being modeled is a counter, choose the Cassandra data type also as Counter. Don't use any other numeric data types.

Getting rid of unwanted records from an RDBMS table is not an automatic process. When application events occur, they have to be removed by application programs or through other means. But in many situations, many data items will have a preallocated time to live. They should go away without the intervention of any external events. Cassandra has a way to assign the **time-to-live** (**TTL**) attribute to data items. By making use of TTL, the data items are removed without any other external event's intervention. This TTL feature is commonly seen in most caching systems.

A brief overview

The concepts such as collection data types, counters, and TTL in Cassandra are very powerful. But before using them to talk about the design patterns, it will be a good idea to discuss some of the basic and general aspects outside the world of Cassandra.

Lists as an abstract idea, occur in our daily life, such as a list of things to buy, a list of tasks to be completed, a list of steps to follow, and so on and so forth. Each of the items in a list has a unique position. Referring to the items in a list by their position happens quite often in our daily conversations, for example, "tell me the first task to be completed", "tell me the high priority item from the list of things to buy", and so on. The items in a list may repeat. For example, the list of steps to follow when driving from point A to point B may have the instruction "Turn Right" repeated many times. However, the position of that step in the list matters. The characteristics of List as an abstract concept are very similar in computer science theory as well.

Sets as a concept, are seen all over the places in our daily life, for example, a set of phone numbers in a phone book, a set of subjects in an examination, a set of emergency contacts in an application form, and so on. A Set is very similar to a List, but there are some fundamental differences. The items in a Set don't repeat. The items in a Set don't have any specific position. The characteristics of a Set as an abstract concept are similar in computer science theory as well.

In general, the items in a Set don't have a unique position in the Set. But there are situations where applications requiring special data types having properties of one or more abstract data types. An ordered Set is one such example, which uses the ordering feature from a List and other features from a Set.

Dictionaries have a very important place in our daily life. They have huge practical applications in every walk of our life. Dictionaries, in the context of books, contain words and their meanings. How do you search for the meaning of a given word in a dictionary? The words are arranged in alphabetical order; you look up the word on the appropriate page and take the meaning given against the word. If you observe closely, you are storing a key and taking the value for that key from the dictionary. This is a very common requirement in many computer applications. In a mathematical sense, it is a mapping from a key to its value. For this reason, this type of abstract data type is called Map in computer science. Map maps a key to its value.

> The abstract data type Map comes with different names in different contexts. Some of these are: an associative array, a symbol table, a dictionary, and a map. The Wikipedia article summarizes this concept very beautifully as follows: "In computer science, an associative array, map, symbol table, or dictionary is an abstract data type composed of a collection of (key, value) pairs, such that each possible key appears just once in the collection."

Data modelers should know this and should choose the column data types judiciously. Different data types are available for different purposes. Many times, the numeric data types are really deceptive. When using a numeric data type, one must know its real use. What is the purpose of that piece of data? Is it used for storing ordinary numeric values? Or is it used for counting purposes? Both these different use cases have a different set of operations on them.

If you know precisely that a specific piece or type of data is going to live only for a known and given period of time, how do you purge it when it completes its lifespan? The data store should give inherent support for this requirement. The TTL attribute of a piece of data defines its end of life from the point of its creation. Wikipedia defines this as:

> *"Time to live (TTL) or hop limit is a mechanism that limits the lifespan or lifetime of data in a computer or network. TTL might be implemented as a counter or timestamp attached to or embedded in the data. Once the prescribed event count or the timespan has elapsed, data is discarded. In computer networking, TTL prevents a data packet from circulating indefinitely. In computing applications, TTL is used to improve performance of caching or to improve privacy."*

List pattern

Whenever a list appears in a real-world use case, use the Cassandra data type the List pattern in the column family. Whenever the list in the real-world use case mandates the order of items, the List data type in Cassandra is ideal. Whenever there is a need to store the same value or object multiple times in the data store, the List data type in Cassandra is the best type to go with.

Motivations/solutions

In the normalized RDBMS tables, whenever there is a need to have a list of things associated with an entity, the easiest, no-brainer approach is to have a one-to-many relationship of two tables. When reports or other business processes need all these pieces of data together, a multi-table join is used. The joins on multiple tables always perform badly when the number of records in the tables are huge. This affects the read performance as well as the write performance. The performance is affected because of two reasons. One, as mentioned earlier, is the need to do table joins, and the other is in the overhead of maintaining indexes on both the tables. Cassandra comes with the data type List that can be used in the column families. This avoids the need to have joins and indexes to keep the related pieces of data together.

Top N queries are very common needs in the applications. To support this requirement, a list of records with proper indexes is maintained in the RDBMS world, and the queries make use of those indexes and serve the results. In RDBMSs, the need to maintain multiple tables exists if there is a master-child or a one-to-many relationship. There is a definite need to have an index whether there is a need to have multiple tables or not. The Cassandra data type List comes in handy in this situation. The items in the list maintain an order. It is this order in which the elements are added to the list.

When choosing List as the data type to store a number of items in the Cassandra column family, make sure that the number of items in the list is not huge. There is no hard limit available on the maximum number of items in the list, but use discretionary judgment on this matter and see how the applications are going to access this list of values, as well as the network bandwidth consumed in transferring the list across multiple Cassandra nodes when processing the lists compiled from multiple rows of the Cassandra column family.

Many-to-many relationships are very common in the real world. It is perfectly possible to model this in the RDBMS, but it is not very natural and intuitive to model this in RDBMS tables. What is meant by this is that there is no one way to do this. Data modelers follow different approaches to solve the many-to-many relationship problem in RDBMSs, and the one most commonly seen is to have one table split into a many-to-one and a one-to-many relation. This is very counterintuitive. In Cassandra, this is a very natural modeling method that makes use of List as the data type in column families. An example is required to elucidate this point. Suppose there is a social networking application where users have followers and users are being followed by other users. Corresponding to each user's record, maintain a list for each of these two categories of users—followees and followers—and the job is over. One might argue that List is not the data type for this use case but it is used here to clarify the point.

Enumeration types are available in many programming languages. This is a list of values and can be accessed using an index. Some RDBMSs support enumeration types as a data type but most of them don't. This is a very common need in many applications. In Cassandra, use the List data type to model enumeration types that arise from the application use cases.

Associated with entities in the real world, there are many attributes that fit properly into a list. Blindly following the RDBMS data modeling rules and splitting them into multiple tables doesn't make sense most of the time because many such lists associated with the entities are small—preferred colors for painting the house, places visited in the past, favorite restaurants, wish list of items to purchase, and so on. If possible, it makes perfect sense to keep all these related lists along with the entities in the data store. In Cassandra, use the List data type in column families and model the entity with as many lists as are needed.

Best practices

List is a very useful and powerful data type in the Cassandra column family. Use it with discretion, especially when the number of items in the list is very large. In such cases, analyze the use case properly, and sometimes it might be sensible to use separate column families to achieve the goal.

The List data type in the Cassandra column family takes a type parameter, such as list of integers, list of strings, and so on. Whenever there is a need to have a list of items with different types, either the List data type is not the appropriate one or the lists can be split based on the data types of the items.

Look at all the characteristics of List as a data type in the Cassandra column family and make sure that the data that is being modeled fits all the requirements. Only then use List as the data type of choice. Ask questions such as, "Do you need to maintain order of items?", "Do you need to store the same item multiple times?", "Do you have different data types for the items in the list?" and so on. If the answers fit the characteristics of a list as a data structure, use the list data type; otherwise look for the right type to represent the data for the use case.

In some cases, there may be requirements to model items in a list with duplicate items that are not allowed. In such situations, if you must maintain the order of the data type in the list, then application logic or business rules must be applied on top of the List data type in Cassandra column families to maintain the business invariant.

It is also very important to look at the operations on the list of items maintained in the Cassandra column family. Even though inserting and deleting items from any position of the list is allowed, careful scrutiny must occur before the decision, to make sure that such operations are not causing any performance problems because of frequent changes to a given record.

Maintaining a sorted list is a requirement in many applications. If the List data type in the Cassandra column family is being used for that purpose, make sure that there is business logic outside Cassandra that is controlling the writes to such lists. There is no direct way to maintain a predefined sort order of items in the list. It is purely the responsibility of the applications to do this because the ordering in the list is not the natural ordering of the element type.

Example

Let's take the example of a `Customer` column family in Cassandra with the columns as shown in the following screenshot:

Figure 1

This column family looks very normal and has a usual structure. But the difference that is being introduced here is in the PasswordHistory column. It is used to store the list of all the passwords that the customer has used in the past. It may contain repeated passwords, so it needs to preserve the order in which they have been used. The List data type containing text values is being used here. By making use of the List data type, all the old passwords are stored in the same column family itself. The CustomerId column is used as the primary key for this column family.

> The Cassandra data type List takes one type parameter. The column with the data type List cannot contain values of multiple data types.

The following script is executed in the cqlsh utility to create the key space and the Customer column family:

```
CREATE KEYSPACE PacktCDP2 WITH replication = {'class':
'SimpleStrategy', 'replication_factor' : 3};
USE PacktCDP2;
CREATE TABLE Customer (
  CustomerId bigint PRIMARY KEY,
  CustomerName text,
  Email text,
  UserName text,
  Password text,
  PasswordHistory list<text>
);
INSERT INTO Customer (CustomerId, CustomerName, Email, UserName,
Password, PasswordHistory) VALUES (1,'George Thomas', 'mt@
example.com', 'mt', 'rret4%6335', ['rret4%6335', 'hrtt5t4%6335',
'rrffer45883635']);
```

The following script shows how the physical records are stored in the Cassandra node. The commands given in this script are to be executed in the Cassandra CLI interface:

```
USE PacktCDP2;

list customer;

Using default limit of 100

Using default cell limit of 100

RowKey: 1

=> (name=, value=, timestamp=1434898063868381)

=> (name=customername, value=47656f7267652054686f6d6173,
timestamp=1434898063868381)
```

```
=> (name=email, value=6d74406578616d706c652e636f6d,
timestamp=1434898063868381)

=> (name=password, value=72726574342536333335,
timestamp=1434898063868381)

=> (name=passwordhistory:795f0db0182411e58643e76149b7842c,
value=72726574342536333335, timestamp=1434898063868381)

=> (name=passwordhistory:795f0db1182411e58643e76149b7842c,
value=68727474357434342536333335, timestamp=1434898063868381)

=> (name=passwordhistory:795f0db2182411e58643e76149b7842c,
value=727266666572343538383833363335, timestamp=1434898063868381)

=> (name=username, value=6d74, timestamp=1434898063868381)
```

1 Row Returned.

In the preceding script, look at the way the `PasswordHistory` column values have been stored. Since it is a collection data type, a unique number has been appended to the column name of the column family to have unique column names. The list has three values, and hence they are represented separately as three separate columns in the physical layout.

The CQL `SELECT` command gives the output in a human-readable format as shown in the following screenshot. Notice the difference in the way the values in the List data type are displayed:

```
SELECT CustomerId as Id, CustomerName, UserName, Password,
PasswordHistory from Customer;
```

```
 id | customername   | username | password  | passwordhistory
----+----------------+----------+-----------+------------------------------------------------
  1 | George Thomas  |       mt | rret4%6335 | ['rret4%6335', 'hrtt5t4%6335', 'rrffer45883635']
```

Figure 2

In a CQL perspective, it will be a good idea to see how to manipulate the values in the List data type. The following script is executed in `cqlsh` to update the contents of the column with the List data type:

```
UPDATE Customer SET PasswordHistory = PasswordHistory +
['xyffer45883635'] WHERE CustomerId = 1;// Add one item to the list
UPDATE Customer SET PasswordHistory[1] = 'xyffer4588upd1' WHERE
CustomerId = 1; //Indexes start from 0. Change the second element of
the list
DELETE PasswordHistory[1] FROM Customer WHERE CustomerId = 1; //Remove
the second element of the list
```

Set pattern

Whenever there is a set in a real-world use case, use the Cassandra data type Set in the column family. Whenever the set in the real-world use case does not mandate the order of items, and if the items don't repeat, the Set data type in Cassandra is ideal. In the applications, even if the duplicate check is relaxed, since the Set data type cannot handle duplicate items, it will not take duplicate items.

Motivations/solutions

In the normalized RDBMS tables, whenever there is a need to have a set of things associated with an entity, the easiest and the most straightforward approach is to have a one-to-many relationship of two tables. When the reports or other business processes need all these pieces of data together, a multi-table join is used. The joins on multiple tables always perform badly when the number of records on the tables is very large. This affects the read performance as well as the write performance. The performance is affected because of two reasons. One, as mentioned earlier,is the need to do table joins, and the other is in the overhead of maintaining indexes on both the tables. Cassandra comes with a data type Set that can be used in the column families. This avoids the need to have joins and indexes to keep the related pieces of data together.

Similarly to what has already been mentioned for the List data type, even in the case of the Set data type, using two Set columns, a many-to-many relationship can be modeled very easily. The only condition is that these records should satisfy all the invariants of the Set data type of the Cassandra column family.

Sets are omnipresent in applications. Take the example of an application user record. In the personal details, it is common to have multiple e-mail addresses, multiple phone numbers, multiple addresses, multiple credit card numbers, and so on. None of these are repeated. In many situations, the order of these items in the data store doesn't matter. Cassandra data type Set is the best way to store them in the column family.

Best practices

Often it is a common requirement to ensure that the values satisfy all the rules of a Set data type, but there will be a need to sort them at the same time. If the number of items in the Set data type-based column is less, it is very easy to do this at the application level.

Set to List and List to Set conversions are very common in applications. They are best done as part of the business logic processing. If it is not overly complex, there is no harm in maintaining the same data in two columns of List and Set types respectively.

The Set data type in the Cassandra column family takes a type parameter, such as a set of integers, a set of strings, and so on. Whenever there is a need to have a set of items with different types, it is because either the data type Set is not appropriate or the sets are split based on the data type of the items.

From Cassandra 2.1 onwards, the creation of secondary indexes on the collection column is allowed. What this means is that you can use CONTAINS in the WHERE clause of CQL. For example, CQL queries such as "SELECT id, name, emails FROM users WHERE emails CONTAINS HYPERLINK "mailto:'gt@example.com'"'gt@ example.com'" is possible if there is a secondary index in the column e-mails.

The creation of secondary indexes on the collection columns has to be done with utmost care. It has advantages, but the performance of reads and writes when the records grow must be taken into consideration.

Example

Let us take the example of a User column family in Cassandra with the columns as shown in *Figure 3*.

Figure 3

The Emails column is a Set data type. It is used to store the set of all the e-mail addresses of the user. It cannot have repeated e-mail addresses. It does not preserve the order in any manner. The Set data type containing text values is being used here. The UserId column is used as the primary key for this column family.

The Cassandra data type Set takes one type of parameter. The column with data type Set cannot contain values of multiple data types.

The following script is executed in the `cqlsh` to create the `User` column family. The assumption is that the key space has already been created using the script for List pattern:

```
CREATE TABLE User (
  UserId bigint PRIMARY KEY,
  UserName text,
  Emails set<text>,
  Password text
);
INSERT INTO User (UserId, UserName, Emails, Password) VALUES
(1,'George Thomas', {'mt@example.com', 'gt@example.com'},
'767gggg22424');
```

The following script shows how the physical records are stored in the Cassandra node. The commands given in this script are to be executed in the Cassandra CLI interface:

```
USE PacktCDP2;

list user;

Using default limit of 100

Using default cell limit of 100

RowKey: 1

=> (name=, value=, timestamp=1435124275686652)

=> (name=emails:6774406578616d706c652e636f6d, value=,
timestamp=1435124275686652)

=> (name=emails:6d74406578616d706c652e636f6d, value=,
timestamp=1435124275686652)

=> (name=password, value=373637676767673232343234,
timestamp=1435124275686652)

=> (name=username, value=47656f7267652054686f6d6173,
timestamp=1435124275686652)


1 Row Returned.
```

In the preceding script, look at the way the `Emails` column values have been stored. Since it is a collection data type, a unique number has been appended to the column name of the column family to have unique column names. The set has two values and hence they are represented separately as two separate columns in the physical layout.

The CQL SELECT command gives the output in a human-readable format as shown in *Figure 4*. Note the difference in the way the values in the Set data type are displayed:

```
SELECT * FROM User;
```

```
 userid | emails                                    | password     | username
--------+-------------------------------------------+--------------+----------------
      1 | {'gt@example.com', 'mt@example.com'}      | 767gggg22424 | George Thomas
```

Figure 4

From a CQL perspective, it will be a good idea to see how to manipulate the values in the Set data type. The following script is executed in the cqlsh to update the contents of the column with Set data type:

```
UPDATE User SET Emails = Emails + {'abc@example.com'} WHERE UserId =
1; // Add one item to the set
UPDATE User SET Emails = Emails - {'abc@example.com'} WHERE UserId =
1; // Remove one item to the set
DELETE Emails FROM User WHERE UserId = 1; // Empty the set
UPDATE User SET Emails = {} WHERE UserId = 1; // Empty the set
```

Map pattern

Whenever there is a need to provide a mapping of keys to values as part of a record, use the Cassandra data type Map in the column family. The "as part of a record" part of preceding sentence is very important. This must not be misunderstood as any general lookup service of records such as the master tables in the RDBMS world.

Motivations/solutions

In the normalized RDBMS tables, whenever there is a need to provide a key to value mapping for an entity, the easiest and most straightforward approach is to create a small lookup table with the key as the primary key of the lookup table and the value as the non-primary key. Just like all the other patterns discussed in this chapter, the joins of the tables are required to get all the pieces of data together even here. All the perils of the table joins are applicable here too. Cassandra comes with a data type Map that can be used in the column families to solve this problem. This avoids the need to have joins and indexes to keep the related pieces of data together.

The need to have a key to value mapping is required in many applications. Right from dictionaries in the real world to the symbol tables in assemblers, we use mapping. Personalization of applications is very common these days. People have lots of preferences, right from the food they eat to the menu placement in their favorite software applications. How do the applications store these preferences? The Cassandra data type Map can be used in the column families to store these kinds of preferences. The preference attribute acts as the key in the Map and the preference value as the value in the Map.

In functional programming languages, transformation functions are very common in the form of regular functions as well as lambda expressions. The function takes an input parameter value, transforms it, and outputs the processed value. In many applications, storing intermediate results in a persistent store is a very common practice. In such situations, it is not uncommon to store the input parameter as key in a Map and the transformed output as the corresponding value. In the analytical use cases, if NoSQL data store such as Cassandra is being used, the Map data type in the column family is ideal for this purpose.

Best practices

As a data structure, bidirectional maps are very commonly used in applications. There is no distinction between the key and the values. In some contexts, this is also called inverse lookup. This is not supported in Cassandra. If required, it is better to maintain two columns with Map as the data type to achieve this. In one column, use the regular key to value mapping, and in the other column, reverse the order and store it as value to key mapping.

Having a huge number of keys in a map is not ideal. For example, it is not appropriate to have one record in the column family with a column having a Map data type, which is used to store a huge number of keys and their corresponding mapping values. In such cases, it is better to use them as a separate and regular column family.

Example

Let us take the example of a Supplier column family in Cassandra with the columns as shown in *Figure 5*:

Figure 5

The `Preferences` column is a Map data type. It is used to store the map of all the preferences of the supplier. The Map data type contains text data contents for both the keys as well as the values. This data structure can store preferences, such as language, currency, and so on, of the supplier. The `SupplierId` column is used as the primary key for this column family.

 The Cassandra data type Map takes two type parameters: one data type for the key and the other data type for the value.

The following script is executed in `cqlsh` to create the `Supplier` column family. The assumption is that the key space has already been created using the script given in *Figure 2*:

```
CREATE TABLE Supplier (
   SupplierId bigint PRIMARY KEY,
   SupplierName text,
   EMail text,
   Phone text,
   Address text,
   ZipCode text,
   Country text,
   Preferences map<text,text>
);
INSERT INTO Supplier (SupplierId, SupplierName, Email, Phone, Address,
ZipCode, Country, Preferences) VALUES (1,'XYZ Inc', 'abc@xyz.com',
'12334537659', 'No 10, Rod Laver Lane, Leeds', 'LS6 1CE', 'UK',
{'Language': 'English', 'Currency': 'Sterling Pound'});
```

The following script shows how the physical records are stored in the Cassandra node. The commands given in this script are to be executed in the Cassandra CLI interface:

```
USE PacktCDP2;
list supplier;
Using default limit of 100
Using default cell limit of 100
RowKey: 1
=> (name=, value=, timestamp=1435266992654659)
=> (name=address, value=4e6f2031302c20526f64204c61766572204c616e652c20
4c65656473, timestamp=1435266992654659)
=> (name=country, value=554b, timestamp=1435266992654659)
=> (name=email, value=6162634078797a2e636f6d, timestamp=1435266992654659)
=> (name=phone, value=3132333334353337363539, timestamp=1435266992654659)
=> (name=preferences:43757272656e6379, value=537465726c696e6720506f756e64
, timestamp=1435266992654659)
=> (name=preferences:4c616e6775616765, value=456e676c697368,
timestamp=1435266992654659)
=> (name=suppliername, value=58595a20496e63, timestamp=1435266992654659)
=> (name=zipcode, value=4c533620314345, timestamp=1435266992654659)


1 Row Returned.
```

In the preceding script, look at the way the Preferences column values have been stored. Since it is a collection data type, a unique number has been appended to the column name of the column family to have unique column names. The map has two values, and hence they are represented as two separate columns in the physical layout.

The CQL SELECT command gives the output in a human-readable format as shown in *Figure 6*. Note the difference in the way the values in the Map data type are displayed:

```
SELECT SupplierId, SupplierName, Preferences FROM Supplier;
```

```
 supplierid | suppliername | preferences
------------+--------------+------------------------------------------------
          1 |      XYZ Inc | {'Currency': 'Sterling Pound', 'Language': 'English'}
```

Figure 6

From a CQL perspective, it will be a good idea to see how to manipulate the values in the Map data type. The following script is executed in the `cqlsh` to update the contents of the column with the Map data type:

```
UPDATE Supplier SET Preferences['Color'] = 'Blue' WHERE SupplierId =
1; //Set a new key/value in the map
DELETE Preferences['Color'] FROM Supplier WHERE SupplierId = 1; //
Remove a new key/value from the map
```

Distributed Counter pattern

Whenever there is a need to maintain counters in applications that need to be persisted and distributed, use the Cassandra Counter data type in the column families. The distributed counter value is 64-bit long, supporting only two operations, namely increment and decrement. This is much better than storing the counter values in RDBMS tables, caches, log files, text files, and so on. In the latest version of Cassandra, the performance of the Counter data type has been improved a lot, and many issues have been fixed to allow it to support very powerful use cases.

Motivations/solutions

The need to use counters exists in most applications. If the application and the database lives in just one node, there is no issue and everything is hunky-dory. The moment any one of these components gets distributed across multiple nodes, the pain begins. Then the need for synchronization arises, and the external synchronization tools such as Zookeeper come into the solution stack. More components are entering the solution stack, and this is not just because of the counting needs, though that might be one of the reasons. The point is that it is not easy to maintain a distributed counter with proper synchronization in a highly distributed application. The Cassandra data type Counter is a perfect fit for this situation. It comes with all the goodies to maintain a completely distributed counter in Cassandra.

 It is very common practice to use sequence numbers as surrogate keys in RDBMS tables. It is not advisable to use the Counter data type in Cassandra to do this. Instead, it is better to use the `TimeUUID` data type.

In traditional RDBMS-based solutions, counters have been used extensively, and it is not very difficult to maintain the sanctity of the counter values. Even if the RDBMS tables are spread across multiple nodes in the same network, counters stored in them do reasonably well. But when there is a need to distribute the RDBMS tables across the data centres, and when the applications have to be scaled out, things start getting really complicated and the solutions become exponentially costly. Cassandra supports multi-data center clusters. The Cassandra data type Counter can be used to store counter values.

The Cassandra data type Counter was introduced in version 0.8.0. Its performance was improved and fixed some of the major issues with it were fixed in version 2.1. The following DataStax Developer post discusses this in detail:

"Cassandra is still one of the only databases that allows race-free increments with local latency across multiple data centres simultaneously, but through Cassandra 2.0 some limitations in the original counters' design continued to cause headaches, notably topology changes potentially leading to bad counters and the infamous invalid counter shard detected problem. These problems and the extra complexity caused by the counters-related special cases in the code base have been fixed in the Cassandra 2.1 release."

The Counter values living in the application session and external caching solutions are very common. These are good ways, but when the applications and the nodes crash, and other faults occur in the system, it can lead to unpredictable consequences. The fundamental problem here is that when the application gets distributed, the data does not get distributed without risks. The Cassandra data type Counter solves all these problems very effectively and efficiently. In other words, reads and writes are very fast, particularly in this context with Counter values, and highly reliable because Cassandra supports multi-data center deployment.

Counting the number of visits on a given web page, the number of transactions, the number of users registered for events, and so on, are very common needs in applications, and if there is such a requirement, use the Cassandra data type Counter. Use it only for counting purposes.

Best practices

The Counter data type in Cassandra columns is different when compared to the other data types. It cannot be used in many situations, and the following are to be given special attention:

- Counter data type columns cannot be indexed
- It cannot be initialized with a given value
- It cannot do any operations other than increment and decrement
- It cannot be used as the primary key
- The TTL property cannot be used with Counter data types

Example

Let us take the example of a website visit statistics application where there is a requirement to capture the number of visits to a given URL for a given date. The following Cassandra column family `WebSiteHit`, shown in *Figure 7*, captures its details. The `URL`, `DateVisited` columns form the primary key. Here, the `URL` column becomes the partition key.

Figure 7

The following script is executed in the `cqlsh` to create the `WebSiteHit` column family. The assumption is that the key space has already been created using the script for List pattern:

```
CREATE TABLE WebSiteHit (
  URL text,
  DateVisited text,
  NoOfVisits counter,
  PRIMARY KEY (URL,DateVisited)
);
UPDATE WebSiteHit SET NoOfVisits = NoOfVisits + 1 WHERE URL='www.
example.com' AND DateVisited='2015-06-27';
```

There are some real differences in the way the Counter values are inserted into a column family. There is no traditional INSERT statement here. Records are inserted using the UPDATE statement.

The physical layout of the rows containing the Counter data type is also slightly different. The following script gives an insight into this. The commands given in the following script are to be executed in the Cassandra CLI interface.

```
USE PacktCDP2;

list websitehit;

Using default limit of 100

Using default cell limit of 100

RowKey: www.example.com

=> (counter=2015-06-27:noofvisits, value=1)


1 Row Returned.
```

The CQL SELECT command gives the output in a human-readable format as shown in *Figure 8*:

```
SELECT * FROM WebSiteHit;
```

```
 url             | datevisited | noofvisits
-----------------+-------------+------------
 www.example.com |  2015-06-27 |          1
```

Figure 8

Purge pattern

Whenever there is a need to remove data after a certain period of time without any external intervention, use the TTL property while inserting records to the Cassandra column family. Instead of depending on the applications or any other external event's intervention, data can be purged off the column family by using the TTL property. The USING TTL clause in CQL can be used to achieve the same. This completely removes the burden from the applications to remove records. Once the time is over, the records are automatically removed from the Cassandra column families. This is very suitable for data items that are short lived in the data store such as session data, cached data, and so on. There are ways to report the time remaining for a piece of data in the data store.

Motivations/solutions

Many web applications store the short-lived session data in memory. This has serious issues if the node crashes or when some system fault occurs. To solve this problem, caching of the session data to some external data store or some external caching solution is very common. Most caching solutions have features to control the life of a piece of data stored in it. If the application is using Cassandra as the data store, there is no need to go for any other caching solution just for storing the short-lived data. Use the USING TTL clause when inserting data into Cassandra column families. If the expected lifetime of the data is only a few seconds, minutes or hours, in many applications the users get an alert on the remaining time-to-live for the data. There is a function, TTL(), that can be used with the column family column names to find out the remaining time-to-live.

Compliance requirements are very common in applications. As per many rules and regulations, a piece of data generated by applications is to be stored only for a certain period of time. After that, it is mandatory to destroy the data beyond recovery. This is a perfect use case where the TTL feature of Cassandra may be used. Once the TTL period is over from the time of its creation, the data is removed from the Cassandra column family.

 The TTL duration for the data items is specified in seconds. The TTL is specified when the data is inserted or updated. If there is a need to change the TTL for a given piece of data, update the data item with a new TTL value.

In online retail applications, it is very common to run promotional campaigns and give offers to loyal customers. In many cases these offers are not valid for eternity; they always come with a deadline. In applications with millions of customers and many offers floating around, it is a huge responsibility for applications to manage this and invalidate the offers extended after the offer period. In such use cases, the TTL feature of Cassandra is a really handy tool to expire the data after a certain period of life.

In many online applications, fraud detection in various shapes and forms is implemented. For example, if a user tries to log in with the wrong credentials, say three times, the account gets locked for 24 hours. Once the 24-hour period is over, the restriction is lifted and the user should be able to try to log in without any manual intervention or without calling a customer service representative. This kind of use case can be implemented with Cassandra's TTL feature for account blocking records.

In many online applications, validating e-mail addresses is a very common requirement when a new account is created. Typically, after the sign-up is completed, the application will send out an e-mail to the registered e-mail ID and give a validity period, say 48 hours, for clicking the link or replying from that e-mail to verify the e-mail ID of the user. This is a perfect use case to use the TTL feature of Cassandra while validating the e-mail ID.

Best practices

The use of TTL must be restricted only to a need-to-have basis. Too many records with TTL are not a good design model, mainly because TTL comes with additional overheads in terms of the main memory and the memory on the disk in addition to the regular data. Apart from that, the server needs to do additional tombstone management work to mark the data after the expiration of the TTL period.

TTL data precision is in seconds. Care must be taken to give a too small TTL number; the data removal need not happen on the precise tick.

It is very important to have the Cassandra cluster with synchronized clocks for small precision TTL to work properly.

Example

Let us take the example of an online web application where the users sign up. Once a user signs up, their e-mail address has to be validated. An e-mail is sent to the registered e-mail ID and the user should click on the URL sent in the e-mail. The following Cassandra column family `EMailVerification` shown in *Figure 9* captures its details. The `UserId` column forms the primary key.

Figure 9

The following script is executed in `cqlsh` to create the `EMailVerification` column family. The assumption is that the key space has been created already using the script for List pattern. The main difference in the script is that while inserting a record into this column family, there is a TTL clause used to remove the record after 2 days of inserting the data. In other words, the users are given 2 days to validate their e-mail ID. If the users don't take any action within 2 days, the record will not be there in the data store and the user will not be able to validate the e-mail address:

```
CREATE TABLE EMailVerification (
   UserId bigint PRIMARY KEY,
   UserName text,
   EMail text,
   ClickURL text,
   DateSent text
);
INSERT INTO EMailVerification (UserId, UserName, Email, ClickURL,
DateSent) VALUES (1,'XYZ Inc', 'abc@xyz.com', 'http://www.example.com/
verify/email/abc@xyz.com', '2015-06-28') USING TTL 172800;
```

The physical layout of the rows in the Cassandra node is given in the following script. The physical layout of the rows containing TTL is slightly different. The TTL values given at the time of the record insertion are shown here. The following script gives an insight into this. The commands given here in the script are to be executed in the Cassandra CLI interface:

```
USE PacktCDP2;
list EMailVerification;
Using default limit of 100
Using default cell limit of 100
RowKey: 1
=> (name=, value=, timestamp=1435527939825148, ttl=172800)
=> (name=clickurl, value=687474703a2f2f7777772e6578616d706c6
52e636f6d2f7665726966792f656d61696c2f6162634078797a2e636f6d,
timestamp=1435527939825148, ttl=172800)
=> (name=datesent, value=323031352d30362d3238,
timestamp=1435527939825148, ttl=172800)
=> (name=email, value=6162634078797a2e636f6d, timestamp=1435527939825148,
ttl=172800)
=> (name=username, value=58595a20496e63, timestamp=1435527939825148,
ttl=172800)


1 Row Returned.
```

The CQL SELECT commands give the output in a human-readable format as shown in *Figure 10*:

```
SELECT UserId, UserName, EMail, ClickURL FROM EMailVerification;
```

userid	username	email	clickurl
1	XYZ Inc	abc@xyz.com	http://www.example.com/verify/email/abc@xyz.com

Figure 10

The CQL SELECT command gives the output in a human-readable format and the remaining TTL for the given row when the CQL command is executed, as shown in the *Figure 11*. Note that when the row was inserted, the TTL given was 172800, and when the following CQL statement in *Figure 11* was given, the remaining TTL for that row was 171463. The elapsed time in terms of seconds has been subtracted from the original TTL number and displayed. When the remaining TTL becomes zero, the row will be marked for deletion, and in the next compaction, the row will be removed from the physical node. In the following CQL statement, the TTL function has been used on the column name EMail, but this can be used on any other column in the same column family. The only constraint is that the column specified must not be the primary key of the column family and must be one of the columns inserted with a TTL clause:

```
SELECT UserId, UserName, EMail, ClickURL, ttl(EMail) as TTL FROM
EmailVerification;
```

The output can be seen in the following screenshot:

userid	username	email	clickurl	ttl
1	XYZ Inc	abc@xyz.com	http://www.example.com/verify/email/abc@xyz.com	171463

Figure 11

Downloading the example code

You can download the example code files from your account at http://www.packtpub.com for all the Packt Publishing books you have purchased. If you purchased this book elsewhere, you can visit http://www.packtpub.com/support and register to have the files e-mailed directly to you.

References

The following links can be referred to for further information:

- https://en.wikipedia.org/wiki/Associative_arrahttps://en.wikipedia.org/wiki/Associative_array
- https://en.wikipedia.org/wiki/Time_to_live"https://en.wikipedia.org/wiki/Time_to_live
- http://www.datastax.com/dev/blog/cql-in-2-1
- http://www.datastax.com/dev/blog/whats-new-in-cassandra-2-1-a-better-implementation-of-counters"http://www.datastax.com/dev/blog/whats-new-in-cassandra-2-1-a-better-implementation-of-counters

Summary

Migrating from RDBMS to Cassandra is a very common requirement in organizations. The preceding chapter and this chapter discussed two important steps: coexistence with RDBMS and migration from RDBMS to Cassandra. The main strategy employed here in the path to migration is by exploiting some of the new and unique features of Cassandra to provide value and to show the quick wins of the migration. The collection data types and the distributed counters help model the applications using Cassandra as the NoSQL data store. The TTL attribute of data in Cassandra column families helps the purging of data that has completed its end of lifespan without any other manual intervention.

Knowingly or unknowingly, caching solutions come to enterprises in the guise of improving the response time of applications. But when that starts playing spoilsport in the ecosystem, mainly resulting in data loss due to various reasons, nobody is happy. In such situations, the best approach is to migrate from such caching solutions to a robust NoSQL data store such as Cassandra, tuned and modeled for fast reads. The next chapter will discuss this.

3
Cache Migration Patterns

"To improve is to change; to be perfect is to change often"

– Winston Churchill

The concept of caching goes back to the very early days of computer architecture. Caching is the process of storing data in an easily accessible store so that requests for the cached data can be fulfilled faster. The Merriam-Webster dictionary defines cache in two ways. In the literal sense, it is defined as:

> *"A group of things that have been hidden in a secret place because they are illegal or have been stolen."*

In the computing sense, it is defined as "a part of a computer's memory where information is kept so that the computer can find it very quickly." Cache is used in both hardware and software. In this chapter, unless otherwise specifically mentioned, all the references to cache refer to cache used in software applications.

In software applications, cache is extensively used to speed up data access. The use of caching mechanisms became very rampant mainly due to the tremendous growth of the Internet and new-generation web applications serving millions of requests per minute. Cache is being used in web applications to serve pages faster. In such cases, either the whole web page or part of the web page is cached. Cache is used to store user preferences in web applications. It is used to store web application session data. It is also used in **Content Delivery Networks (CDN)** to serve static contents such as audio, video, and other heavy-weight or rich media contents. In CDNs, the content that needs to be served fast is stored in the same geographical region where most of the users are located. Cache is used heavily in searching. It is used in the **Domain Name System (DNS)** to provide lookup to translate a DNS name into its IP address. In all of these caching examples, the required data is served from the caching solution instead of the traditional persistent data stores.

Database access, whether it is from RDBMS or other highly distributed NoSQL data stores, is always an **input/output (I/O)** intensive operation. It makes perfect sense to cache the frequently used but reasonably static data for fast access to the applications that consume that data. In such situations, in-memory cache is preferred over repeated database access for each request. Some databases support a feature called **query caching**. In this method, if a specific query is being used frequently, the results of that query are stored in the in-memory data structures to provide fast responses. The results of complex calculations derived from various data sources are cached in many applications.

There are very specific terms that are unique to caching. For example, cache hit, cache miss, and so on are some of the commonly used terms related to caching. Wikipedia gives a nice and concise description about cache, and some of the commonly used terms related to cache, as follows:

"In computing, a cache is a component that stores data so future requests for that data can be served faster; the data stored in a cache might be the results of an earlier computation, or the duplicates of data stored elsewhere. A **cache hit** *occurs when the requested data can be found in a cache, while a* **cache miss** *occurs when it cannot. Cache hits are served by reading data from the cache, which is faster than recomputing a result or reading from a slower data store; thus, the more requests can be served from the cache, the faster the system performs."*

The most commonly seen incarnation of a cache comes in the form of a key/value pair store, so any piece of data should be morphed into the key/value format before it is stored in the cache. There are some caching solutions that support much more than key/value pairs. They support generic data structures, such as list, set, map, and so on. Many RDBMSs allow in-memory storage of the exact replica of RDBMS tables.

Cache is used to store data that is difficult to access otherwise. Some examples of this are the data that is read from an RDBMS or from some legacy data stores that are expensive to access in terms of the time required or the resource requirements, such as the need to make repeated connection requests to the data source.

Cache is used to store data that is needed by the clients (as in software) quite frequently. Some examples of this are the most commonly used datasets by applications, such as configuration file contents, lookup table contents, and so on.

Object/Relational Mapping (ORM) solutions are used to map the underlying RDBMS table records to objects in applications. ORM solutions such as **Hibernate** are used heavily in Java-based applications. ORM solutions use caching. There are various strategies used to read data from the underlying RDBMS tables and cache it in-memory.

Most caches use the main memory to store their contents. Some of them use only main memory to store the cache contents, while some of them use an overflow strategy such that when the size grows beyond a threshold, the contents are overflown to a persistent store, and some of them maintain an exact copy of the cache contents in the persistent store. Many caching solutions use one kind of data eviction strategy or another to keep the size of the cache in check. The main memory is not infinite, and there should be some strategy to remove the contents from the cache to keep its size under control. Discarding the earliest used items first, discarding the most recently used items first, discarding the least frequently used items first, and so on are some of the commonly seen data eviction strategies employed by caching solutions.

 Scaling out by distributing to multiple nodes as a cluster is a very common method used to avoid single points of failure in any system. Caching solutions are not different. Many caching solutions can be distributed across multiple nodes.

Using the cache is not always a pleasant experience. Getting into really weird problems, such as data loss, data getting out of sync with its source, and other data integrity problems, is very common. The next section is going to be a brief overview of the problems that are commonly seen when using cache.

A brief overview

When data is being served rapidly for read requests from the already existing caching solution, why migrate from such a caching solution to a NoSQL data store such as Cassandra? Having mentioned what cache is and some of the common use cases of cache, we will now cover some of the perils of using cache. It is very common to see the wrong components entering an enterprise solution stack all the time, for various reasons. Overlooking some of the features, adopting a technology without much background work is a very common pitfall. Initial evaluations go fine, but once the development is completed, bumping into an unforeseen problem is very common. Many times, some products come in as a suite and using them without a strong case is seen very often. Organizational politics has its unique place in making some really bad decisions regarding technology.

Many times, cache is used in the solution stack to reduce the latency of responses. Once the initial results are favorable, more and more data will get tossed into the cache. Slowly, this will become a practice to see that more and more data is getting into the cache. This is the time problems start popping up one by one. Pure in-memory cache solutions are everybody's favorite by virtue of their ability to serve data rapidly, until you start losing data because of faults in the system, application crashes, and node crashes. This is even more dangerous if there is no persistent store, such as an RDBMS table, backing up the cache. In other words, the contents of the cache exist only in the in-memory cache. This can be due to the absence of the right configuration to make the data persist, or the caching system in use might not support persistence in a durable medium. In such situations, if you lose the data in the cache, it is a clean case of data loss.

> In a cache, it is ideal to have a key (if it is a string) of moderate length. This means that the key should not be too short, because the number of key/value pairs that can be stored in a cache will be limited. The key should also not be too long because then searching the key in cache becomes cumbersome. Often these are some of the reasons why a cache doesn't perform well.

Cache poisoning, or dirty contents in cache, is another cause of concern. There is an RDBMS table or some other persistent store where the data resides and cache is employed to speed up responses. Now, if for some reason the underlying data changes and if this is not reflected in the cache contents in a timely manner, this becomes a serious data integrity issue. This is mainly applicable to cache backed by a persistent data store and the case when the data changes frequently.

Data management is a very important aspect in all data stores. There should be proper tools to manage the data apart from the programming interfaces. There should also be a proper hierarchy in which data can be stored, namely a namespace. Many caching solutions don't have a concept of namespace. In other words, the data is thrown into a black box. You have no idea what is in there. When you try to retrieve, it will give the data if it exists in the cache, and a null value otherwise. In such situations, it is very difficult to organize the data properly. Think of an RDBMS where there is no schema and table definition at all. Namespaces are required for all data stores. RDBMSs have the database and table as namespace abstractions. Some NoSQL solutions have bucket types and buckets as namespace abstractions. Cassandra has the key space and column family/table as namespace abstractions. Without a proper namespace abstraction built into the cache system, maintaining the data will become a nightmare.

Whether it is cache, RDBMS, or NoSQL data stores, the availability of data management tools is very important. This includes tools for defining as well as manipulating data. A large number of caching solutions don't have many data management tools. They just expose the interfaces to put data into it, get data from it, and delete data from it.

How do you make sure that the cache and the underlying data store are in sync with the production systems? There is no hard-and-fast rule to enforce this. But resorting to running non-intruding and asynchronous random tests is one of the best ways of spotting and reporting such errors. Randomly picked-up items from the cache are compared with their source. Anomalies are logged to take corrective measures. It is better to build this capability in the application itself as business logic so that the application becomes self-correcting. This reduces a lot of problems. Cassandra employs many self-correction mechanisms very effectively to maintain the integrity of the data in its column families.

Lack of cache coherence is another problem seen in many caching solutions. From a common data store, multiple caches are built; and if, for some reason, one or more caches are out of sync with the source, the coherence is lost. Wikipedia gives a good account on the cache coherence like this:

"In a shared memory multiprocessor system with a separate cache memory for each processor, it is possible to have many copies of any one instruction operand: one copy in the main memory and one in each cache memory. When one copy of an operand is changed, the other copies of the operand must be changed also. Cache coherence is the discipline that ensures that changes in the values of shared operands are propagated throughout the system in a timely fashion."

Even though the preceding description is in the context of cache in computer architecture, the same concept holds well in software caches too. When Cassandra is used in place of a caching system, applications read data from the column families, and there is no question of the need to maintain multiple copies of the same piece of data. Hence, cache coherence is achieved automatically.

Cache to NoSQL pattern

Cache serves data much faster than that being served from other data stores. But if the caching solution in use is giving data integrity problems, it is better to migrate to NoSQL data stores, such as Cassandra. Is Cassandra faster than in-memory caching solutions? The obvious answer is, "No". But it is not as bad as many think. Cassandra can be configured to serve faster reads, and the bonus comes in the form of high data integrity with strong replication capabilities. The Cassandra read path starts with the checking in of the bloom filter. It is a probabilistic method of seeing whether the requested data is present in a given SSTable or not, before getting into the I/O operations. If the bloom filter gives a favorable nod, the next step is to check in the partition key cache. If the key is found, the row is returned. If the key is not found, the SSTables are read, and when data is available, it is merged, sorted, and returned. There are ways to cache an entire row in the memory for faster reads.

> The Cassandra documentation has great coverage of caching strategies. The most important point related to caching is this:
>
> *"Typically, you enable either the partition key or row cache for a table, except archive tables, which are infrequently read. Disable caching entirely for archive tables."*

Motivations/solutions

Lookup tables, name/value pairs or key/value pairs coming from properties files, and so on are commonly stored in cache. These are the simplest cases of using cache. Migrating these to Cassandra is very easy. Create column families with exactly the same structure as in the cache, and the job is done.

> Cassandra 2.1 introduced a data type called **Tuple**. This holds fixed-length sets. Each of the elements in the set has a definite data type. The fields in the tuple are position aware. For example, a tuple can be defined as `tuple<text, int, float>` to represent the name, age, and weight of a person entity in the form, for example, `'Roger Federer', 33, 75`. This has a lot of applications as it is very easy to keep related information in a position-aware fashion without the pain of explicitly defining it as a data type. In applications that process Cassandra data, transformations can be done very easily because the contents are strongly typed too.

Cache is used in many ways. The critical factor is the content of the cache. As mentioned earlier in this chapter, most cache implementations are with a key/value pairs of data. The key will typically be a primitive data type, such as numeric types or string types, but the value comes in all sorts of flavors of primitive as well as non-primitive data types. In many cases, it will be a big chunk of string data, such as **Extensible Markup Language (XML)** data, **Java Script Object Notation (JSON)** data, raw text data, and so on. If a cache-to-Cassandra migration is taking place for any of these big chunks of string data, these structures can potentially be mapped directly to Cassandra column families, where the key will be the sole primary key and the other column will hold the string value data. This is an exact one-to-one migration from a cache to Cassandra. It need not be done in this way. There are better ways to do it. See whether the big lump of text contents in the form of XML or JSON can be properly categorized into any of the collection data types, such as list, set, map, or tuple. Say, for example, if the big text chunk is a JSON string containing a couple of lists, sets, maps, tuples, and string values. One approach is to store the key of the cache as the primary key and then define multiple columns with these different Cassandra data types. The advantage of storing the data is to bring a structure to the stored data, which is not achieved when it is stored as XML or JSON.

Cassandra 2.1 introduced a new data type called **User-defined Type (UDT)**. Using UDT, multiple pieces of related data can be combined together to define a new data type. Suppose there is a need to store a list of locations as part of a Cassandra column family. The location should have a city name and longitude and latitude values. In this case, a new data type called `Location` can be created with `city`, `longitude`, and `latitude` as the fields. A new UDT is created using the CQL statement `CREATE TYPE`. It can be changed with `ALTER TYPE` and can be dropped with `DROP TYPE`.

Dealing with big chunks of values in a cache is a challenge. The challenge is even greater when it is being migrated to Cassandra. Different from many other NoSQL data stores, Cassandra favors storing highly structured data in its column families. Take the same case of a JSON string stored as a value in a cache and assume that it is being migrated to Cassandra. In contrast to the discussion before, if the option to split the big chunk of the JSON string into its constituent primitive and collection data types is not feasible because of the need to have all the pieces of data together for the applications consuming the data, the next alternative is to create a UDT equivalent of the structure of the JSON string. Even in this case, there is an assumption that the data conforms to a very strict and firm structure modeled by he UDT.

Content delivery networks and audio/video streaming applications use cache extensively. In the cache used for such purposes, the value will typically contain rich media. In other words, they are arbitrary bytes for other applications. If there is a need to migrate from the cache to Cassandra with the cache holding rich media or other arbitrary bytes, the Cassandra data type blob can be used to hold such data.

There is a major misconception that the contents of the cache must reside in the main memory all the time. Often, the need to have a caching strategy may be to store some intermediate results of a business rule process that is otherwise not available directly from the data store. In many situations similar to this, such semi-processed results will end up in the cache. Usually, these intermediate results will be used only a few times, and the eviction of such contents from the cache takes place as per the configured eviction policy.

A good example of this would be the high-value transaction alert service that is part of many banking products. Whenever a high-value transaction occurs in a given account, the customer is notified by e-mail, SMS, and so on as per the settings made by the customer or by the bank. When a transaction occurs, a business rule check is done to see whether the transaction qualifies as a high value transaction. If it does, then it is copied to a cache and some other process takes care of alerting the customer. Once the customer is notified, this record will be processed by another business process, such as fraud detection. These records will be retained in the cache for a while longer, maybe for correlation purposes or to monitor whether any more such transactions occur in quick succession. There are arguments for and against the need for a cache in this case. But the point is that in some situations like this, there is no real need to have an in-memory cache to store these records. Cassandra column families, designed for fast reads, will serve that purpose. If there is a need to remove the records from Cassandra column families, the TTL feature also comes in handy, which will automatically remove the records after the specified lifetime when inserting the record.

The cache must be configured properly to serve the data in an effective way. It cannot hold the data indefinitely in the main memory. So, a proper eviction policy must be employed. In some cases, for a certain set of data, if the policy is first-in-first-out, and for other sets of data, the policy is last-in-first-out, and possibly can have more policy requirements. There will be practical difficulties in implementing multiple eviction policies for different sets of data items. In this situation, keep only the most appropriate data items in the caching system to have a proper eviction policy in use, and others can be migrated to Cassandra.

Best practices

When you are dividing a big lump of text data of a value in cache to proper data types in Cassandra column families, care must be taken to make sure that all the possible values in the cache strictly follow a given structure. If the text data is a free-form kind of text that comes in various sizes and formats, then it is better to maintain it as a single column in the Cassandra column family.

When you are using UDT as the data type in the Cassandra column families, validation must be done from the application itself to make sure that the data that is getting inserted into the Cassandra column family conforms to the contract for the UDT.

Multiple rounds of performance tuning must be done before the cache is migrated to Cassandra in order to perform well. This depends a lot on the data and the way applications were using the cached data before migrating to Cassandra.

Example

Let's take the example of a JSON value stored in a cache. Corresponding to every customer code as a key in the cache, a JSON value containing the customer details and the order details is stored. The following script shows the JSON structure:

```
{
  "CustomerCode": "CS001",
  "CustomerName": "Mike Thomas",
  "Email": "mt@example.com",
  "Address": "No.3, Park Avenue, Leeds, LS4 1B8, UK",
  "Phone": "+44756678588",
  "Orders": [
    {
      "OrderId": 245,
      "OrderDate": "2015-01-20",
      "OrderAmount": 1250.50
    },
    {
      "OrderId": 557,
      "OrderDate": "2015-04-25",
      "OrderAmount": 5200.00
    }
  ]
}
```

Now this is going to be converted into a Cassandra column family with exactly the same structure. The CustomerCode column will be the sole primary key, and hence it will be the partition key as well. There is a list of orders for a given customer record. The Orders record will be defined as a UDT in Cassandra. The following block of code shows the script used to create the CustOrder UDT and the Customer column family. This script is executed in the cqlsh utility:

```
CREATE KEYSPACE PacktCDP3 WITH replication = {'class':
'SimpleStrategy', 'replication_factor' : 3};
USE PacktCDP3;
CREATE TYPE CustOrder (
  OrderId bigint,
  OrderDate text,
  OrderAmount float
);
CREATE TABLE Customer (
  CustomerCode text PRIMARY KEY,
  CustomerName text,
  Email text,
  Address text,
  Phone text,
  Orders list<frozen<CustOrder>>
);
INSERT INTO Customer (CustomerCode, CustomerName, Email, Address,
Phone) VALUES (
  'CS001',
  'Mike Thomas',
  'mt@example.com'
  'No.3, Park Avenue, Leeds, LS4 1B8, UK',
  '+44756678588'
);
UPDATE Customer SET Orders = [{OrderId: 245, OrderDate: '2015-01-
20', OrderAmount: 1250.50}, {OrderId: 557, OrderDate: '2015-04-25',
OrderAmount: 5200.00}] WHERE CustomerCode = 'CS001';
```

In the preceding script, first the key space is created. Then, the UDT for the CustOrder customer order is created. Next, the Customer column family is created, and finally the record is inserted.

 The frozen keyword, when used in conjunction with UDT, is for making sure that the UDT value cannot be updated in parts.

The following script shows how the physical records are stored in the Cassandra node. These commands are to be executed in the Cassandra CLI interface:

```
USE PacktCDP3;
list Customer;
Using default limit of 100
Using default cell limit of 100
RowKey: CS001
=> (name=, value=, timestamp=1435867051450377)
=> (name=address, value=4e6f2e332c205061726b204176656e75652c204c656564732
c204c5334203142382c20554b, timestamp=1435867051450377)
=> (name=customername, value=4d696b652054686f6d6173,
timestamp=1435867051450377)
=> (name=email, value=6d74406578616d706c652e636f6d,
timestamp=1435867051450377)
=> (name=orders:cb36714020f411e5aab89d03f52e8a2b, value=000000
0800000000000000f50000000a323031352d30312d323000000004449c5000,
timestamp=1435867145806604)
=> (name=orders:cb36714120f411e5aab89d03f52e8a2b, value=000000
08000000000000022d0000000a323031352d30342d32350000000445a28000,
timestamp=1435867145806604)
=> (name=phone, value=2b3434373536363738353838,
timestamp=1435867051450377)
```

1 Row Returned.

The CQL SELECT command gives the output in a human-readable format, as shown in the following screenshot, and shows the way the UDT values are displayed:

```
SELECT CustomerCode, Orders FROM Customer;
```

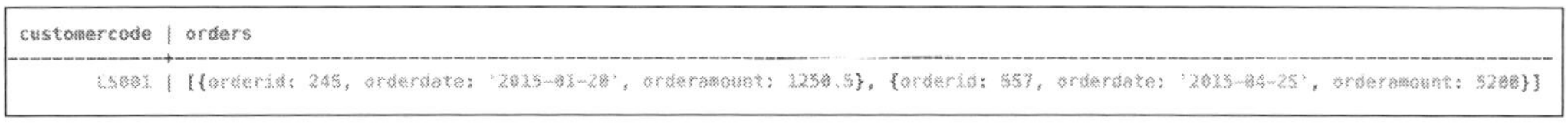

Figure 1

References

The following links can be referred to for further information:

- https://en.wikipedia.org/wiki/Cache_(computing)
- https://en.wikipedia.org/wiki/Cache_coherence
- http://docs.datastax.com/en/cassandra/2.1/cassandra/operations/ops_configuring_caches_c.html

Summary

Continuing on the migration strategies, migration from cache to Cassandra was discussed in this chapter. Cache is good as long as it serves its purpose without any data loss or any other data integrity issues. Emphasizing on the use case of the key/value type cache, various methods of cache-to-NoSQL migration were discussed. Cassandra cannot be used as a replacement for cache when it comes to speed of data access. But when it comes to data integrity, Cassandra shines all the time with its tunable consistency feature. With continual tuning and manipulation of data with clean and well-written application code, data access can be improved a lot, and it will be much better than many other data stores.

Consistency, availability, and partition tolerance are three important guarantees that any distributed computing system should offer, even though all three of these might not be possible simultaneously. Depending on the way data is ingested into Cassandra and the way it is consumed from Cassandra, tuning to give the best results for the appropriate read and write requirements of the application is possible. The next chapter will discuss this.

4
CAP Patterns

"Your Coffee Shop Doesn't Use Two-Phase Commit"

– Gregor Hohpe

Those who have worked on database applications will be familiar with **two-phase commit**. Whenever there are multiple application elements or components in a distributed system, there are two phases in order to perform an atomic transaction. In the first phase, all the participating components have to say "yes" for the transaction. If all of them say "yes," then in the second phase the changes have to be committed, which completes the transaction. This is an oversimplified description of the two-phase commit.

> A transaction is said to be **atomic** if it cannot be divided further. There is another way to interpret this: If there are multiple steps in a given transaction, either all the steps complete successfully, or none of them completes.

Even if the systems are distributed, if the number of components is very small, a two-phase commit doesn't affect the response time of the requests. But when it comes to large scale Internet applications, or the large scale web services popularly known as **Internet of Things (IoT)** applications, the quantity of components is huge, and the way they are distributed is beyond imagination. There will be hundreds of application servers and hundreds of data store nodes and many other components in the whole ecosystem. In such scenario, doing an atomic transaction by getting agreement from all the components involved is for all practical purposes impossible. In other words, the two-phase commit in an IoT application is practically impossible.

The IoT applications are highly distributed. Most of the IoT application functionalities or services are mission critical, for example, financial transactions, shopping cart services, real-time monitoring services, and so on. The consistency of the data is important—the C part. From a Cassandra perspective, consistency refers to how up-to-date a piece of data item is across all the replicated nodes. The availability of the service is important—the A part. From a Cassandra perspective, when client applications write or read data, availability refers to how Cassandra is serving those requests so that client the operation can be completed as fast as possible. The services must be network partition tolerant—the P part.

 When Cassandra nodes are deployed across multiple data centers or multiple racks, it is very common that network connectivity issues, or in other words, network partition, occur. In such situations, how tolerant Cassandra is in serving the read and write requests is referred by network partition tolerance.

It is really a balancing act to provide all the **C**, **A**, and **P** guarantees (generally referred to as **CAP**) for a given application or service. In an IoT application, it is theoretically and practically impossible to have a 100 percent guarantee on all the three CAP parts. This is the very problem that Eric Brewer conjectured as CAP Theorem. According to Brewer, it is possible to give a guarantee on only two from the three CAP guarantees. According to this theorem, if an IoT application is to give Consistency and Availability, then it cannot be distributed, and hence network Partition Tolerance guarantee cannot be given. If Availability and network Partition Tolerance are given, then the Consistency cannot be guaranteed. If network Partition Tolerance and Consistency are given, then the Availability cannot be guaranteed. Later on, Seth Gilbert and Nancy Lynch went on to prove that what Brewer conjectured is true.

In the IoT applications, distribution of the application nodes is unavoidable. This means the possibility of network partition is very much there. So, it is mandatory to give the P guarantee. Now, the question is whether to forfeit the C guarantee or the A guarantee. At this stage, the situation is not as grave as portrayed in the CAP theorem. For all the use cases in a given IoT application, there is no need of having 100 percent of C guarantee and 100 percent of A guarantee. So, depending on the need of the level of A guarantee, the C guarantee can be tuned. In other words, it is called tunable consistency.

In Cassandra, consistency levels can be tuned. The Cassandra documentation says the following:

> *"Consistency levels in Cassandra can be configured to manage availability versus data accuracy. You can configure consistency on a cluster, data center, or individual I/O operation basis. Consistency among participating nodes can be set globally and also controlled on a per-operation basis (for example insert or update) using Cassandra's drivers and client libraries."*

In some of the IoT application use cases, it is necessary to have fast writes. In that case, if the writing is going to verify that the data is written to all the nodes, where the data is replicated, to make sure that the data is consistent across all the nodes, the write operation will be slow and the availability will be less. So, the best way to solve this problem is to make sure that the write operation is not going to do the consistency check across all the nodes. This cannot be done blindly. So, to make sure that there is no consistency issue with the data, it is necessary while reading the data to make sure that it is reading from multiple nodes and that they are consistent. In this case, the reading operation's availability will be less, but this is fine.

In some of the IoT application use cases, it is mandatory to have fast reads. In that case, if the reading operation is going to check all the nodes where the data is replicated, to make sure that the data is consistent across all the nodes, the read operation will be slow and the availability will be less. So, the best way to solve this problem is to make sure that the read operation is not going to do the consistency check across all the nodes. But again, this cannot be done blindly. So, to make sure that there is no consistency issue with the data, it is necessary while writing the data to make sure that it is written in multiple nodes without any errors. In this case, the writing operation's availability will be less, but this is fine.

There is a class of IoT application use cases where both the write operations and the read operations should be equally fast. In this case, it cannot be as fast as described in the write-fast and read-fast use cases. Some compromise on availability will have to be made.

A brief overview

How are we going to control the consistency of the read and write operations in Cassandra? For this, it is important to take a look at the tuning parameters available in Cassandra and see how these parameter values affect the writes and reads in the Cassandra nodes.

In a cluster of Cassandra nodes, a row in a column family is replicated on multiple nodes as per the replication factor setting. When a write takes place, it is first written onto the co-ordinator node, and eventually replicated onto the other nodes, and only then will the data that has been written be consistent across all the nodes. A client writing data into Cassandra column family need not wait until the data that is written onto one node is replicated in all the replica nodes. In such cases, there are many ways to make sure that the data is consistent across all the nodes even when the client is not waiting for the confirmation from all the nodes after the write operation. One of them is a proactive method—AntiEntropy and the other is a reactive method—Read Repair.

> While setting the read or write consistency levels in a client program, the concept of QUORUM is very important. Assume that there are two data centers, *DC1* and *DC2*, where the Cassandra cluster is distributed. Assume that the replication factors of Cassandra cluster in these two data centers are *DC1_RF* and *DC2_RF* respectively. In that case, the value of *QUORUM = ((DC1_RF + DC2_RF)/2) + 1*. Suppose that the read or write is taking place from *DC1*, then *LOCAL_QUORUM = (DC1_RF /2) + 1*.

The client programs can control the consistency of a write operation in Cassandra. The following list of consistency levels is given in the order of the highest to the lowest write consistency levels (ALL to ANY where; ALL being the highest level of consistency and ANY being the lowest level of consistency) that can be set by a client program writing data to a Cassandra column family:

- ALL
- EACH_QUORUM
- QUORUM
- LOCAL_QUORUM
- THREE
- TWO
- ONE
- LOCAL_ONE
- ANY

Here in the case of write, if the consistency level is the highest, then the availability will be the lowest. If the consistency level is the lowest, then the availability will be the highest.

Similarly, the client programs can control the consistency of a read operation in Cassandra. The following list of consistency levels is given in the order of the highest to the lowest read consistency levels (ALL to LOCAL_ONE; ALL being the highest level of consistency and LOCAL_ONE being the lowest level of consistency) that can be set by a client program reading data from a Cassandra column family:

- ALL
- EACH_QUORUM
- QUORUM
- LOCAL_QUORUM
- THREE
- TWO
- ONE
- LOCAL_ONE

 Note that there is no ANY in the read consistency levels when compared to the write consistency levels. There are two other consistency levels, namely SERIAL and LOCAL_SERIAL, which are used exclusively in the light weight transactions. These cannot be configured as a consistency level by the client programs at the driver level.

Here in the case of read, if the consistency level is the highest, then the availability will be the lowest. If the consistency level is the lowest, then the availability will be the highest.

In terms of the consistency levels that can be set by the client programs, the consistency and the availability can be controlled in both write and read operations.

 As per Cassandra documentation, if consistency is really important, then it has to be made sure that *(nodes_written + nodes_read) > replication_factor* and it is briefly notated as *(W + R) > N*.

In the case of operations where the read and write are equally important, the consistency level setting by the client programs play an important role. It is the responsibility of the client programs to make sure that sum of the number of nodes into which the data is written and number of nodes from which the data is read is greater than the replication factor. This is to make sure that more nodes are consulted either at the read level or at the write level and that the data is in a consistent state.

Since the tips and tricks of controlling the consistency and availability are now covered, it makes sense to get into the discussion of the application needs with respect to the reads and writes. In some applications, the speed at which the data is written will be very high. In other words, the velocity of the data ingestion into Cassandra is very high. This falls into the write-heavy applications. In some applications, the need to read the data fast will be of an important requirement. This is needed mainly in the applications where a lot of data processing is required. Data analytics applications, batch processing applications, and so on fall under this category. These fall into the read-heavy applications. Now there is a third category of applications where there is an equal importance to fast writes as well as fast reads. These are the kind of applications where there is a constant inflow of data, and at the same time, a need to read the data by the clients for various purposes. This falls into the read-write balanced applications category.

The consistency level requirements for all these three types of applications are totally different. There is no one way to tune so that it is optimal for all the three types of applications. All three applications' consistency levels need to be tuned differently according to use case.

All these consistency levels change a lot when the replication factor changes, when the number of Cassandra nodes changes (whether increasing or decreasing), when the nodes are distributed across multiple racks or data centers, and when the node layout changes. So it is not as easy as to make the consistency level changes once and freely change the Cassandra node deployment layout as per the need. It is very important to note that the consistency level settings are to be evolved as and when the Cassandra node deployment is evolved. It should be a continual improvement process. So, performance monitoring, reporting, and fine tuning are required on a regular basis to make sure that the application performance is at its best. Some best practices can be followed, but since the use cases are totally different from application to application, a one-size-fit-all strategy cannot be applied to give the right level of consistency and availability to the applications. Hence, the design patterns discussed in this chapter are just some guidelines, and the application designers have to use their own discretion based on their application behavior to arrive at the best configuration and get the best performance.

> Wherever the consistency level settings given in this chapter are more than ONE, it is important to make sure that the number of alive nodes in the cluster is greater than or equal to the consistency level setting. For example, if you have a single node Cassandra setup and if you are trying the CQL scripts given in this chapter where there is a consistency level setting THREE, the CQL commands will fail.

Write-heavy pattern

In an IoT application with Cassandra as the data store, if the inflow of the data is very high, the write consistency levels should *not* be set high. Consistency levels of ANY, LOCAL_ONE, and ONE are ideal. The data comes in with a high velocity, and the data store should work like a sink. In this situation, if the consistency levels are set high, then for each write, the clients have to wait until the write is completed successfully on the required number of nodes as per the consistency level setting. The complexity increases when there are Cassandra clusters spread across multiple data centers in a network operations perspective. When the clients wait for the write to complete because of high consistency level settings, the availability will be lesser, and the efficiency to complete the writes will also become lesser. This, in turn, increases the latency, and the overall application performance will be affected. It is also ideal to avoid secondary indexes in the Cassandra column families where a huge number of writes are taking place.

Motivations/solutions

There is no dearth of IoT applications that receive the input data at high velocity. Real-time applications are aplenty. The data comes in the form of real-time live data feeds, data streams, batch updates to data stores, and so on. Cassandra is a good NoSQL data store to store the data coming with high velocity. Thanks to the tunable consistency feature of Cassandra, the consistency settings can be made at the client level itself to make sure that the large scale data ingestion can be honored. In many cases, the applications can directly write the data to Cassandra, and in many other cases, an intermediary service such as a cache can be employed to write the data first and then delegate the write from there to Cassandra if data ingestion velocity is very high and appropriate consistency levels can be set for the write operations of Cassandra.

Very popular online games generate lots of data. These data can have a huge variety as well. The data include player preferences, current state of the game, scores, historic data, and so on. Many popular online games are played by thousands of players at a given point in time. In these situations, it is very important to have all the data points stored in the data store in a timely manner. Any kind of delay, or any kind of failure to store the data may cause user experience issues. Many online game service providers use Cassandra as their preferred data store.

Software as a Service (SaaS) is one of the important cloud service models where fully functional applications are offered as a service. In this type of service offered by the service providers, one application instance will be running in most of the cases that will be shared by multiple users with a very strict isolation of the data and other resources following the rules of multitenancy. Some social media applications are examples of this type of SaaS applications. They generate lots of data in various formats. In the case of applications shared by millions of users at a given point in time, the amount of data that is getting written is really huge. Instantaneous writes is a must for most such applications. Because of this, Cassandra is used in many such SaaS applications.

There is another kind of SaaS application provider where primary user interface is through mobile applications. These mobile applications generate lots of data such as photos, text messages, audio, and video. In this case, some of the data types fall into rich media and are difficult to transfer because of their huge size. When such data is written into a data store, there are many challenges. Many of the RDBMS struggle to deal with this set of variety of data types and the huge velocity at which it is coming to the data store. Cassandra can be used to store these kinds of data, mainly because it supports a large number of data types and the write operation can be made faster by tuning its consistency parameters.

Online betting exchanges generate huge amounts of data. The specific nature of these exchanges is in a way such that the sports events happen in a completely uncoordinated manner. So in such sites, there will be a sudden flurry of transactions coming in, and the applications have to ingest a lot of data with the lowest possible amount of latency. Many times, this type of spikes in the transaction volume will amount to a huge number without adhering to a specific scheduled working hours. In other words, the transactions take place in a 24x7 manner without any predictability. In such situations, the write performance of the applications is very important. Each of the transactions is very important. No loss of transaction is tolerated. Cassandra can be used to receive this kind of data with a tuning set to have low consistency and high availability levels.

Best practices

When using the consistency levels in Cassandra for writes and reads, it is important to maintain the balance of $(W + R) > N$. In this situation, the W number is going to be less in order to provide fast writes. So there should be some mechanism to have at least some applications do read with high consistency levels to maintain this consistency relation.

It is also common to write the high-velocity data coming into a cache first and then some other program taking data from the cache and write into Cassandra with high-consistency levels so that the applications writing the data are not blocked, and at the same time very high consistency level is maintained. Care must be taken while adopting this strategy because it is of paramount importance to manage the cache in such a way that it does not result in inconsistent state at any given point in time.

If third-party applications are allowed to write data into the Cassandra data store, only the **Application Programming Interfaces (API)** are to be exposed, and the consistency level setting must be encapsulated within the exposed API. In other words, the exposure to setting consistency level must not be given to the third-party applications interacting with the Cassandra nodes. The main reason why this has to be done at API level is because if third-party applications do not adhere to the consistency level suggested, then there is no way to guarantee the consistency of the write operations.

It is important to pay attention to the consistency level setting to make sure that the number of alive replicas are greater than or equal to the consistency level setting. For example, if the consistency level setting is THREE and the number of alive replicas is ONE, then the operation will fail with an error message similar to the following:

```
""Cannot achieve consistency level THREE" info={'required_replicas':
3, 'alive_replicas': 1, 'consistency': 'THREE'}"
```

It is also a common practice to choose machines with **Solid State Disk (SSD)** when the storage media for the Cassandra nodes with high volume writes are happening. Such machines will give a better performance when compared with the machines with spinning disks.

Example

Let's take the example of a gaming application Spaceship where the users play online. The Cassandra column family Spaceship shown in the following screenshot captures its details. The columns UserId and ActionTime constitute the primary key. The UserId column becomes the partition key.

Figure 1

The following script is executed in the cqlsh to create the key space and Spaceship column family:

```
CREATE KEYSPACE PacktCDP4 WITH replication = {'class':
'SimpleStrategy', 'replication_factor' : 3};
USE PacktCDP4;
CREATE TABLE Spaceship (
   UserId bigint,
   ActionTime timestamp,
   UserName text,
   Coordinates tuple<int, int>,
   Score int,
   GameOver boolean,
   PRIMARY KEY (UserId, ActionTime)
);
```

Now the key space and the column family are created, as per the usual practice. The Spaceship column family is a write-heavy column family as many concurrent users are playing the game online and their space ship movements are captured in this column family. So, the writes have to be extremely fast, and hence the consistency has to be relaxed to achieve this. The consistency level is at a protocol level. In other words, the consistency level is not set at an individual CQL command level. Set the consistency level; until that is changed, all subsequent CQL commands executed will have that consistency level.

If a Cassandra client library is used, instead of CQL, for inserting data in a programmatic manner, the consistency level has to bet set at the driver level.

The following script is to be executed in the `cqlsh` to set the consistency level. Once this is done, insert the record into the `Spaceship` column family with the lowest consistency level to facilitate a high write availability:

```
CONSISTENCY ANY;
INSERT INTO Spaceship (UserId, ActionTime, UserName, Coordinates,
Score, GameOver) VALUES(1, dateof(now()), 'Benjamin Thomas', (120,
340), 56, false);
```

The following script shows how the physical records are stored in the Cassandra node. These commands are to be executed in the Cassandra CLI interface:

```
USE PacktCDP4;

list customer;

Using default limit of 100

Using default cell limit of 100

RowKey: 1

=> (name=2015-07-14 20\:24+0100:, value=, timestamp=1436901897110397)

=> (name=2015-07-14 20\:24+0100:coordinates,
value=00000004000000780000000400000154, timestamp=1436901897110397)

=> (name=2015-07-14 20\:24+0100:gameover, value=00,
timestamp=1436901897110397)

=> (name=2015-07-14 20\:24+0100:score, value=00000038,
timestamp=1436901897110397)

=> (name=2015-07-14 20\:24+0100:username, value=42656e6a616d696e2054686f6
d6173, timestamp=1436901897110397)


1 Row Returned.
```

The CQL `SELECT` command is shown here. Since the `ANY` consistency level is not supported for read operations, the consistency level has to be changed to a high value to get high consistency.

```
CONSISTENCY THREE;
SELECT * FROM Spaceship;
```

The following *Figure 2* shows the output of the preceding command in a human-readable format:

userid	actiontime	coordinates	gameover	score	username
1	2015-07-14 20:24:57+0100	(120, 340)	False	56	Benjamin Thomas

Figure 2

To check the consistency level set at present, execute the following command at the `cqlsh` prompt and it will display the consistency level as shown in the following command:

```
CONSISTENCY;
Current consistency level is THREE.
```

Read-heavy pattern

In an IoT application with Cassandra as the data store, if the number of reads is higher when compared to the writes, the read consistency levels should not be set high. Consistency levels of `LOCAL_ONE`, `ONE` are ideal. In this case, the data store works like a source. In this situation, if the read consistency levels are set high, then the clients will have to wait for each read until the read is completed successfully from the required number of nodes as per the consistency level setting. The complexity increases when there are Cassandra clusters spread across multiple data centers. When the clients wait for the read to complete because of high consistency level settings, the availability will be less and the efficiency to complete the reads will also decrease. This, in turn, increases the latency, and the overall application performance will be affected. It is also ideal to have secondary indexes in the Cassandra column families where a huge number of reads are taking place with `WHERE` clauses on non-primary keys.

Motivations/solutions

Many of the social networking sites expose APIs for third-party applications to read posts and other contents. For example, Facebook implemented Cassandra for their inbox search system. Messages in Facebook-like applications are huge in size, and the amount of read taking place from such a system is also huge. Apart from Facebook itself using these APIs to display on the pages, there are various other APIs available that can be used by anybody to access the messages and the like. In such situations, the read must be very fast, and the only way to achieve this is by making sure that the read consistency levels are kept low so that the availability is high.

Financial trading exchanges expose APIs for third-party applications to query on the trade positions. Trade positions are binding agreements to buy or sell instruments such as stocks. Yahoo! Finance is a good example of such a third-party application, which reads the stock trading information from financial trading exchanges, does many complex calculations on them, and publishes stock quotes through their website. In other words, Yahoo! doesn't own or generate these data. Rather, they read from the financial exchange data through the APIs exposed by these institutions. Here, we have talked about one third-party that is Yahoo!, but there can be thousands of such "Yahoos" accessing the data from those financial trading exchanges. If Cassandra is used to store the trading positions data as discussed here, it is a very strong use case of high volume reads, and has to be served with very low latency. In such cases, the Cassandra column families are to be designed for fast reads, and thus, the consistency levels of the client programs should be set low so that the availability will be high.

Microblogging is a concept that has become popular in the recent years and there are some very popular platforms that let users publish blogs in a totally unconventional way. Instead of writing big article such as blog posts, the users can share blog posts in the tune of a few sentences. Such platforms also allow users to share audio, video, and so on. This is one of the most modern ways of blogging as it makes a lot more people feel inclusive in the blogging culture. It is very difficult to draw a demarcation line between these microblogging sites and other social networking sites, but one thing is sure that the number of users reading these microblogs are much greater than the number of people who read traditional blogs. As a result of this, the number of users doing read operations from these sites is really huge. The main use case is reading. So, if the data store for which this kind of microblogging applications are built is Cassandra, it is very important to provide capability to read data from these data stores with high availability. High availability for read means low read consistency. The client programs should be designed in such a way that the consistency levels are set very low to provide high availability.

Weather reporting is a huge application area. Many websites report weather predictions. Many mobile applications provide weather forecast. Most of this weather forecast data is not being served from the origin of the data. Many such application providers store the relevant precalculated data in their servers as per the format mandated by their application. So, in many organizations the weather data is stored, and the data stores are designed to serve for fast reads by the applications of the APIs exposed by them. It is very critical to provide fast reads from these data stores. Cassandra is a great data store for data that is dedicated for high volume reads due to its tunable consistency parameters that can be set at the client level to provide high availability.

Mobile applications and web applications reporting live sports events with real-time scores are very common. These applications report the scores with minimal time delay in comparison to watching a live event. Such applications have to serve data for really fast reads as the number of users ramp up when popular sports events take place, such as tennis grand slam finals, major football matches, and so on. Cassandra is a good fit to host such real-time data for fast reads.

Best practices

The consistency levels for reads have to be set at the client programs reading the data from Cassandra, but if this is left to the end users, as in the case of the financial trading exchanges, there is no guarantee that the third-party applications will adhere to the consistency-level recommendations. Since this is the case, it is better to have a wrapper application that uses low consistency level to provide high availability. Once this is done, expose only such APIs to the third-party, instead of giving direct access to the Cassandra data store.

It is important to pay attention to the consistency level setting to make sure that the number of alive replicas are greater than or equal to the consistency level setting. For example, if the consistency level setting is THREE and the number of alive replicas is ONE, then the operation will fail with an error message similar to the following:

```
""Cannot achieve consistency level THREE" info={'required_replicas':
3, 'alive_replicas': 1, 'consistency': 'THREE'}"
```

It is also common practice to choose machines with SSD as the storage media for the Cassandra nodes while high volume reads are taking place. Such machines will give a better performance in comparison to the machines with spinning disks.

There is an in-memory option for Cassandra column family to serve fast writes and reads, but this is not available in the open source version of Cassandra; it is available only in the DataStax Enterprise 4.x onwards. Care must be taken while using this option, mainly because of the data size limit in the memory cache. A proper flushing strategy must be employed to make sure that the data is not lost forever. The DataStax Enterprise documentation must be consulted before using this feature.

Cassandra documentation gives some valuable guidelines on setting the client consistency levels as follows:

"You can use a new cqlsh command, CONSISTENCY, to set the consistency level for queries from the current cqlsh session. The WITH CONSISTENCY clause has been removed from CQL commands. You set the consistency level programmatically (at the driver level). For example, call QueryBuilder.insertInto with a setConsistencyLevel argument. The consistency level defaults to ONE for all write and read operations."

Example

Let's take the example of an online microblogging application `Microblog`, where the users read blog entries online. The Cassandra column family `Microblog` shown in the following screenshot captures its details. The columns `UserId`, `ActionTime` constitute the primary key. The `UserId` column becomes the partition key.

Figure 3

The following script is executed in the `cqlsh` to create the `Microblog` column family. It is assumed that the key space has already been created:

```
CREATE TABLE Microblog (
  UserId bigint,
  ActionTime timestamp,
  UserName text,
  BlogTitle text,
  Content text,
  Visible boolean,
  PRIMARY KEY (UserId, ActionTime)
);
```

Now, the key space and the column family are created as per the usual practice. The `Microblog` column family is a read-heavy column family as many users are reading the online microblog posts from this column family. So, the writes have to be extremely consistent and can afford to have low availability. However, the reads have to be extremely fast, and hence the consistency levels have to be relaxed.

The following script is executed in the `cqlsh` to set the consistency level. Once this is done, insert the record into the `Microblog` column family with the highest consistency level to facilitate a high write consistency:

```
CONSISTENCY ALL;
INSERT INTO Microblog (UserId, ActionTime, UserName, BlogTitle,
Content, Visible) VALUES(1, dateof(now()), 'Benjamin Thomas',
'Cassandra Design Patterns', 'Cassandra is the best columnar store',
false);
```

The following script shows how the physical records are stored in the Cassandra node. These commands are to be executed in the Cassandra CLI interface:

```
USE PacktCDP4;

list microblog;

Using default limit of 100

Using default cell limit of 100

RowKey: 1

=> (name=2015-07-14 22\:22+0100:, value=, timestamp=1436908927028565)

=> (name=2015-07-14 22\:22+0100:blogtitle, value=43617373616e647261204465
7369676e205061747465726e73, timestamp=1436908927028565)

=> (name=2015-07-14 22\:22+0100:content, value=43617373616e6
472612069732074686520626573742020636f6c756d6e61722073746f7265,
timestamp=1436908927028565)

=> (name=2015-07-14 22\:22+0100:username, value=42656e6a616d696e2054686f6
d6173, timestamp=1436908927028565)

=> (name=2015-07-14 22\:22+0100:visible, value=00,
timestamp=1436908927028565)


1 Row Returned.
```

The CQL `SELECT` command is shown here. The consistency level has to be changed to a low value to get high availability.

```
CONSISTENCY ONE;
SELECT * FROM Microblog;
```

The following *Figure 4* shows the output in a human-readable format:

```
 userid | actiontime             | blogtitle                | content                      | username       | visible
--------+-------------------------+--------------------------+------------------------------+----------------+--------
      1 | 2015-07-14 22:22:07+0100 | Cassandra Design Patterns | Cassandra is the best columnar store | Benjamin Thomas |   False
```

Figure 4

Read-write balanced pattern

In an IoT application with Cassandra as the data store, if the amount of write and the amount of read is balanced, then it is a tricky situation. It is difficult to have high availability for write as well as read. So, the best way to handle the situation is to go with the formula $(W + R) > N$. In other words, the sum of the number of nodes written and the number of nodes read is greater than the replication factor. It is also common to have two different but replicated clusters of Cassandra nodes, and in that, one is optimized for fast reads and the other for fast writes. But this has to be done with caution and the main reason is because once the data is written into one cluster, how fast that should be available for read from the other cluster. It is purely a business-rule-based requirement and there is no hard-and-fast rule that can be applied.

Motivations/solutions

Many of the financial transactions are highly read-write balanced patterns. This is commonly seen, especially in real-time systems. Here, typically a transaction that is written decides the behavior of the next transaction, and hence a read before the next write is required. For example, take the case of a retail banking transaction. If a person is continuously withdrawing money from an **Automatic Teller Machine (ATM)**, it is important to have the balance updated immediately after each withdrawal. In this case, the write has to be fast because of the high availability needs; and, at the same time it is also important that read is also fast because a balance check is required before each withdrawal. Since many of the NoSQL data stores such as Cassandra are eventually consistent, often this withdrawal transaction is performed in different steps in such a way that the available balance is updated as quickly as possible, and the transaction record is written later. A reconciliation job is run later to make sure that the available balance is sound. The key here is to write the transaction records with very high consistency and make sure that none of them is lost by any chance. Typically, this is done in an asynchronous manner so that the client programs are not waiting for the job to complete.

Again, there is no standard way in which this is done; the take-away concept here is that many of the financial transactions are read-write balanced and the appropriate consistency levels are different from case to case. Cassandra can be tuned to have a read-write balance and used for the read-write balanced transactions.

Many scientific computations depend on complex formulae, and they are completed after running many iterations of the computations. When there are multiple iterations, in many situations the iterations have to be improvisation iterations. In other words, do one iteration of computation, use the computed value, and feed it into the next iteration, and so on and so forth. In such situations, if the results of the iterations are written into NoSQL data stores such as Cassandra, the writes and reads have to be extremely fast to make sure that the iterations are getting completed fast. The complexity increases when there are concurrent programs doing the writes and the reads. Here, both the writes and the reads have to be highly available. The amount of high availability depends on the application. Cassandra is suitable to have read-write balanced applications, such as the one described here, doing iterative computing tasks.

In most auction sites and applications, the writes and reads are equally important and have to be highly available. When an auction is open, auctioneers will be bidding, and until the auction process is completed, the bidding will continue. The general nature of bidding is such that a bid depends on the previous bid. So the order of transactions coming in, the writes, and the reads are equally important. Cassandra is designed for fast writes, fast reads, and a balanced use of both.

Best practices

To provide fast writes and fast reads, care must be taken, if two clusters are designed, to constantly monitor the transactions and continually improve the consistency levels to get the optimal performance. There is no one way to get the right performance for all the use cases.

In many use cases, even if the non-functional requirements suggest that both the reads and the writes have to be highly available, the $(W + R) > N$ formula will work just fine most of the time for the application. Wherever possible, it is safe to use this if it gives the right level of performance.

When tuning for fast writes and fast reads, make sure that in the beginning the consistency levels for both writes as well as reads are set high. For example, set a **QUORUM** consistency level for both writes and reads in a single data centre, Cassandra cluster. Then, based on the requirements and performance, relax one to get the final relation $(W + R) > N$ right.

Example

Let's take the example of a retail banking transaction application `RetailBank` where the transaction entries are written and read with equal importance. The Cassandra column family `RetailBank` shown in the following screenshot captures its details. The columns `CustomerId`, `ActionTime` constitute the primary key. The `CustomerId` column becomes the partition key.

Figure 5

The following script is executed in the `cqlsh` to create the `RetailBank` column family. It is assumed that the key space has already been created:

```
CREATE TABLE RetailBank (
   CustomerId bigint,
   ActionTime timestamp,
   CustomerName text,
   TransactionType text,
   Amount double,
   PRIMARY KEY (CustomerId, ActionTime)
);
```

Now, the key space and the column family are created as per the usual practice. The `RetailBank` column family is a read-write balanced column family as many transactions are being written into it and many applications are reading them from this column family. So, the writes and reads have to be balanced.

The following script is executed in the `cqlsh` to set the consistency level. One this is done, insert the record into the `RetailBank` column family with the balanced consistency level to facilitate a high write consistency:

```
CONSISTENCY QUORUM;
INSERT INTO RetailBank (CustomerId, ActionTime, CustomerName,
TransactionType, Amount) VALUES(1, dateof(now()), 'Benjamin Thomas',
'D', 1250.50);
```

The following script shows how the physical records are stored in the Cassandra node. These commands are to be executed in the Cassandra CLI interface:

```
USE PacktCDP4;

list retailbank;

Using default limit of 100

Using default cell limit of 100

RowKey: 1

=> (name=2015-07-15 19\:28+0100:, value=, timestamp=1436984933204072)

=> (name=2015-07-15 19\:28+0100:amount, value=40938a0000000000,
timestamp=1436984933204072)

=> (name=2015-07-15 19\:28+0100:customername, value=42656e6a616d696e20546
86f6d6173, timestamp=1436984933204072)

=> (name=2015-07-15 19\:28+0100:transactiontype, value=44,
timestamp=1436984933204072)


1 Row Returned.
```

The CQL SELECT command is shown here. The consistency level has to be changed as a performance tuning exercise to get optimal user experience:

```
CONSISTENCY QUORUM;
SELECT * FROM RetailBank;
```

The following *Figure 6* shows the output in a human-readable format:

customerid	actiontime	amount	customername	transactiontype
1	2015-07-15 19:28:53+0100	1250.5	Benjamin Thomas	D

Figure 6

 In this chapter, wherever a consistency level setting was done, it was only indicative and not prescriptive. Depending on the use case, they will have to be tuned. In the preceding examples, various consistency levels such as ONE, ANY, QUORUM, ALL, and so on were used, which can be changed as per the requirement.

References

The following links can be visited for further information:

- `http://www.enterpriseintegrationpatterns.com/docs/IEEE_Software_Design_2PC.pdf`
- `http://www.infoq.com/articles/cap-twelve-years-later-how-the-rules-have-changed`
- `http://webpages.cs.luc.edu/~pld/353/gilbert_lynch_brewer_proof.pdf`
- `http://docs.datastax.com/en/cassandra/2.1/cassandra/dml/dml_config_consistency_c.html`
- `https://wiki.apache.org/cassandra/AntiEntropy`
- `http://wiki.apache.org/cassandra/ReadRepair`
- `https://www.facebook.com/notes/facebook-engineering/cassandra-a-structured-storage-system-on-a-p2p-network/24413138919`
- `http://www.datastax.com/wp-content/uploads/2014/02/WP-DataStax-Enterprise-In-Memory.pdf`

Summary

In this chapter, various design patterns related to applications with the needs of fast writes, fast reads, moderate writes, and moderate reads were discussed. All these design patterns revolved around using the tunable consistency parameters of Cassandra. Whether it is for write or read, if the consistency levels are set high, the availability levels will be low, and vice versa. So, by making use of the consistency level knob, the Cassandra data store can be used for various types of writing and reading use cases.

In any application, usage of data that varies over time, also called **temporal data**, is very important. Temporal data is needed wherever there is a need to maintain chronology. There are many applications in which there is a huge need for storage, retrieval, and processing of data that is tied to time. The next chapter will discuss some of the use cases with temporal data, and how Cassandra is well-made for such purposes.

5
Temporal Patterns

"Time is not a line, but a series of now-points"

–*Taisen Deshimaru*

Time is the most important attribute of any event. Without the time attribute, no event has any meaning. It is not just the time occurred; there are many other time-related attributes in an event. Events change state over a period of time, and all these points of time where there is a change of state become part of the event. Together, they become individual time attributes. These time attributes are used to perform a lot of analyses, processing, and reporting activities related to the events. In this case, if an event is considered as a data point, time is part of this data point.

There is another class of data points that change over a period of time, known as **temporal data**. Whenever these data points are captured, it is mandatory to capture the related time as well. In other words, these data points don't have an independent existence without the associated time. Some of the commonly seen examples of temporal data include weather stations reporting the temperature and humidity at a given location, stock exchanges reporting the price of a given stock, and so on. These data points change all the time.

The biggest challenge in dealing with temporal data stored in a data store is that they are largely used for analytical purposes and for retrieving the data based on various sort orders in terms of time. So, the data stores that are used to capture the temporal data should be capable of storing the data by strictly adhering to the chronology. It can be in either ascending order of time or descending order of time. The two-pronged challenges here are the storage of the temporal data while preserving the order of time and the retrieval of the temporal data as per the desired sort order. Considering the volume of data that is getting ingested into the data stores, retrieving all the data in a data store in one shot is practically impossible.

So, the next obvious choice is to retrieve a part of the data that is captured in the range of a time period. The query that is used to retrieve the data in a range of values is generally known as the **range query**. The ideal data store supporting temporal data should handle the storage and retrieval of data very effectively to support range queries. From a data store perspective, a data store can handle temporal data effectively if it can store the data in the desired sort order of time, retrieve the data in the desired sort order of time, and effectively support range queries between the desired intervals of time with at least a millisecond precision. This is not a hard and fast rule, but it is a very common requirement.

In most present day data stores, time is recorded with respect to the epoch time. Wikipedia defines an epoch as follows:

> *"In the fields of chronology and periodization, an epoch is an instant in time chosen as the origin of a particular era. The 'epoch' then serves as a reference point from which time is measured. Time measurement units are counted from the epoch so that the date and time of events can be specified unambiguously.*
>
> *Events taking place before the epoch can be dated by counting negatively from the epoch, though in pragmatic periodization practice, epochs are defined for the past, and another epoch is used to start the next era, therefore serving as the ending of the older preceding era. The whole purpose and criteria of such definitions are to clarify and co-ordinate scholarship about a period, at times, across disciplines."*

In Cassandra, timestamp-related data types are stored as 64-bit signed integers representing a number of milliseconds since the the epoch, which is January 1, 1970 at 00:00:00 GMT. The **Epoch Time** is also known as **Unix Time**, or **POSIX Time**. All the timestamps before the epoch are stored as negative integers and the timestamps after the epoch are stored as positive integers.

When it comes to the precision of the timestamp, most systems store the timestamp with millisecond precision. The obvious question would be: given that these days it is very common to have a need to store the timestamps in microsecond and nanosecond precision, why are most of the data stores not inherently supporting that level of precision? There are two reasons for this. The first is that many of the existing programming languages don't support nanosecond precision in their library, and the second reason is that many of the data stores don't have data types supporting nanosecond precision.

In Cassandra, things are going to change for good in terms of storing nanosecond precision timestamps. Java 8 has a time API that has nanosecond precision, and in the future versions of Cassandra, the timestamp data type is going to have nanosecond precision.

In many systems where there are a huge number of concurrent writes happening, if timestamps are used as the primary key or part of the primary key, there is a possibility of collision because of the timestamps having only millisecond precision. As a result of this, there is a possibility of data loss or failure to store the data into the data store because a record has already been written with the same timestamp. For example, if two records are being written with timestamp keys having the same millisecond level, but differing in a microsecond or nanosecond level, then the second record write will fail. In such situations, it is better to use a combination of a timestamp and some other unique identifier for the primary key, as this resolves timestamp-related collisions. Data stores should have inherent support for such collision-free insertion of temporal data without the clever use of client program libraries or a cookbook approach to the data store features.

In Cassandra, there is a data type timeuuid that can be used for collision-free writes of temporal data. The Cassandra documentation gives a detailed explanation about the usage of this data type as follows:

> *"Timeuuid types can be entered as integers for CQL input. A value of the timeuuid type is a Version 1 UUID. A Version 1 UUID includes the time of its generation and are sorted by timestamp, making them ideal for use in applications requiring conflict-free timestamps. For example, you can use this type to identify a column (such as a blog entry) by its timestamp and allow multiple clients to write to the same partition key simultaneously. Collisions that would potentially overwrite data that was not intended to be overwritten cannot occur."*

From a purely theoretical perspective, temporal data has a bitemporal attribute. Bitemporality can be easily explained with an example of event data. A bitemporal attribute consists of two time attributes: the **Valid Time** and the **Transaction Time**. Valid Time represents the time when the real-world event happened, and the transaction time represents the time when the event was stored in the data store. To elucidate this point, suppose that a banking transaction occurred on Sunday, July 19, 2015, 11:27:30. If the entry is stored in the data store at Sun Jul 19 2015 11:27:31, then the first one is the Valid Time and the second one is the Transaction Time. Other than these two temporal attributes, there can be multiple timestamp-related attributes for the temporal data. Apart from this, there are many more definitions and features that are needed for an ideal temporal data store, such as time period data type, bitemporal relations, more specific predicates for querying time periods, and so on. There are many products in the market claiming that they support many such theoretical features; but in most applications, it is not practical to go to such selective, narrow focused products just to store temporal data. Ideally, the data store should support all the basic needs of the data storage and retrieval engine, and on top of that, it should support temporal data management as well.

Cassandra cannot be classified as a pure temporal data store according to the theoretical definition of a temporal database. It is a highly powerful, industry-strength NoSQL data store with some great battle-tested features to handle temporal data in an optimal way, and is being used to power many IoT applications.

Another misconception that is seen commonly is that the terms "time series" and "temporal data" are used interchangeably. There is a subtle difference here. Time series captures a series of data items over a time interval. Here, "time interval" is a very important part. The only commonality is that, in time series, there is a temporal ordering of the data. The data points don't have any natural ordering per se, unless they are tied to a timestamp. For example, a set of stock prices captured independent of the time at which those prices were applicable does not have any natural order; that is, these numbers 31.50, 32.50, 33.50, 30.00 as stock prices don't make any sense as they don't have any natural order. But the tuples capturing the stock prices and the associated timestamp at which those prices are valid give more meaning to those prices and have a natural order; hence it qualifies to be temporal data {(31.50, Mon Jul 20 2015 11:30:00), (32.50, Mon Jul 20 2015 11:35:00), (33.50, Mon Jul 20 2015 11:40:00), (30.00, Mon Jul 20 2015 11:45:00)}.

When talking about time series, an important point to consider is the concept of time interval. Many of the temporal data stores abstract the time period as a data type. This data type has a start timestamp and an end timestamp supporting a lot of algebraic relations popularly known as **Allen's Interval Algebra**.

Cassandra does not have a time period data type. If it is a must, the Cassandra UDT might be used to define a new data type with a start timestamp and an end timestamp. In the future versions of Cassandra, **User Defined Functions (UDF)** are going to come. Cassandra UDT, in conjunction with Cassandra UDF, may be used to serve the needs of time period data type in Cassandra. In other words, you can define a time period data type using UDT and implement all the functionality needed to use that UDT using UDF.

A brief overview

There are many usage patterns seen in the real world that show temporal behavior. For the purpose of classification, in this book they are bucketed into three categories. The first is the general time series category. The second is the log category such as in an audit log, a transaction log, and so on. The third is the conversation category such as in conversation messages of a chat application. There is relevance in this classification because these are commonly used across many applications. In many applications, these are really cross-cutting concerns and designers underestimate this aspect. And also many of the applications will have different data stores capturing this temporal data. There is a need to have a common strategy dealing with temporal data that falls in these three commonly seen categories in an enterprise-wide solution architecture. In other words, there should be a uniform way of capturing and processing temporal data, and there should be a commonly used set of tools and libraries to manage the temporal data.

Even though the three classifications discussed previously are taken as different use cases, they have very common behavior in a tools and processing method perspective. But the idea of this chapter is to consider these three classifications separately, and this will give the effect of dealing with three use cases, which then will make it easy to identify other temporal data-related use cases in various applications and device a strategy to manage that effectively in a generic way.

Time series data is seen everywhere. They are collected with the associated timestamp and used later for various analysis purposes. In the IoT applications, there is one more dimension to this type of data. They get ingested into the data store with very high velocity in many use cases. In any temporal data, timestamp is an inevitable attribute; but how to store them is a very important consideration. If the application use cases need them in ascending order, store them in ascending order of time. If the application use cases need them in descending order, store them in descending order of time.

Many types of logs are ubiquitous in all kind of applications. Each of these log entries has a timestamp. From an enterprise perspective, if all the log entries are taken collectively, most of them will have different contents and formats. As a result of this, getting a big picture on performance and troubleshooting applications is getting complex day by day. In many situations, these log files are transferred to a common location and then analysis is performed or some monitoring tools are employed to track the contents of the logs. Because of these complexities, enterprise-wide common log repositories are seen very commonly these days. When the log entries from various sources are getting collected into a NoSQL data store such as Cassandra, they have a clear behavior of temporal data because of the log entries' sensitivity to the time of occurrence as well as chronology.

Application use cases falling into the conversation behavior are very common. For instance, online chat used in social networking applications, customer relationship management applications, and so on have this conversational behavior. Messages from various systems come into a common sink with an associated timestamp. They have to be processed by various applications in the same order they happened or in reverse order. There is a huge applicability for this type of use case in social media applications, service management applications, and event management applications. In general, conversation messages come into the data store with an associated timestamp.

In the RDBMS or any other legacy data stores, if the tables are designed with proper relation, there is not much to do and applications are free to access them in any desired order to process them. But when it comes to the storage of temporal data in NoSQL data stores such as Cassandra, careful consideration should be given in selecting the appropriate keys suitable for writes and reads. Partition keys have to be selected with great care because high-velocity data comes in, and if the wide row capacity is exhausted, this will lead to many complexities, such as data loss.

Graphing libraries or business intelligence applications are the major consumers of temporal data. Many graphing packages expect the data in a certain format. The slicing and dicing of the data as per the needs of the applications have to be thought through in the very beginning itself. Unlike RDBMS, NoSQL data stores don't extend the freedom to retrieve the data in any desired order.

Out of the three design patterns that will be discussed here, the first Time Series pattern is a general design pattern that covers the most general behavior of any kind of temporal data. The next two design patterns, namely Log pattern and Conversation pattern, are two special cases of the first design pattern.

Time series pattern

In an IoT application with Cassandra as the data store, a time series can be modeled with the timestamp or timeuuid data types in conjunction with an appropriate data type for the data points. Corresponding to each data point, a time data type is to be used. In this design pattern, a timestamp or timeuuid data type column must not be used as the single partition key because there will be only one data point per row. There should be at least one associated timestamp or timeuuid for each of the data points. It is ideal to choose a meaningful partition key so that the Cassandra CQL queries return data points in a given period without reading multiple rows. It is ideal to store all the most commonly needed records in one big row if possible as this will make the data access faster. Since Cassandra stores the data points in a column family in the sorted order as per the partition key, primary key, and clustering column specifications, the retrieval pattern must be decided early on during the data modeling stage itself.

Motivations/solutions

Time series use cases are seen very commonly in many of the application use cases. They come in many different shapes and forms. Time series data is used heavily in statistics. One of its most common use is for trend analysis. For example, in the case of population data, trend analysis can be used to see whether the population is consistently increasing or decreasing over time. In this case, the population data is captured for many date/time instances and plotted to analyze the trend. Here, for every population number, there will be a corresponding date/time value, making it a time series. Cassandra can be used to store this time series data, and also for many other trending and analysis purposes.

There is a huge applicability of time series in various signal-processing applications. Signals modeled with amplitude data points corresponding to time values are used in many applications these days. Various transformations such as Fourier transform are applied on these signal time series. Audio, video, and image manipulations can be performed with such time series data. Cassandra is a great NoSQL data store to store such time series data.

Many financial trading data falls into the time series category. In a financial trading exchange, the stock trades taking place during the trading window and the data generated are perfect example of time series data. Some of the important elements of each transaction include the stock symbol, transaction type, transaction time, number of stocks, and stock price. These sets of data points can be modeled as a time series. Cassandra is being used by many of the financial trading applications to capture real-time and high-volume time series data.

The cash withdrawal transactions taking place in an ATM and the data generated by those transactions fall into the time series category. The account number, amount, and transaction time combination is another example of time series data. Cassandra, with its great capabilities to handle time series data, is a great NoSQL data store, and is being used by many IoT applications.

Best practices

It is very important to properly model time series data in the first place so that many unforeseen problems related to data storage, data access, and row runout issues can be avoided later. In any time series modeling effort, the following decisions are to be made after carefully study of the application behavior. As the NoSQL gurus say, decide the application behavior and then do the data modeling, not the other way around.

- **Partition key**: Select this properly by understanding that, for every distinct value of this, there will be a new row in Cassandra.

- **Primary key**: A combination of a Partition key with or without another column(s), a Primary key will determine a unique record in Cassandra.

- **Clustering order**: This will decide the sort order in which the records are stored physically on the disk of a Cassandra node.

- **Number of records**: By having a careful look at the Partition key, Primary key, Clustering order, and the specificity of the use case, estimate the number of records, and make sure that they don't exceed the capacity of a wide row in Cassandra.

In a specific time series data, if the millisecond precision of a timestamp data type is not sufficient, use the timeuuid data type instead. The need comes when the data ingestion is huge and there is a chance of having multiple data points with microsecond or nanosecond precision for the same millisecond number. In such cases, collision takes place and data loss occurs.

Example

Let's take the example of a banking application ATMWithdrawals, where the customers withdraw money from ATM and only these transactions are captured in this column family. The Cassandra column family ATMWithdrawals shown in the following screenshot captures these details. The columns CustomerId and ActionTime constitute the primary key. The CustomerId column becomes the partition key. The records are stored in the descending order of the ActionTime. This is to make sure that the recent transactions are accessible first. In a time series perspective, it is a good idea to know how many records there will be per row.

For every customer, there will be one row and all the transaction records will be in the same wide row. However great the number of transactions from the same customer, it will never exceed the capacity of one wide row in Cassandra, which is 2 billion cells per partition.

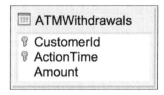

Figure 1

The following script is executed in the `cqlsh` to create the key space and `ATMWithdrawals` column family:

```
CREATE KEYSPACE PacktCDP5 WITH replication = {'class':
'SimpleStrategy', 'replication_factor' : 3};
USE PacktCDP5;
CREATE TABLE ATMWithdrawals (
   CustomerId bigint,
   ActionTime timestamp,
   Amount double,
   PRIMARY KEY (CustomerId, ActionTime),
   )WITH CLUSTERING ORDER BY (ActionTime DESC);
```

Now, the key space and the column family are created as per the usual practice. The `ATMWithdrawals` column family is designed to hold a time series data. The following script is executed in the `cqlsh` to insert three records into the `ATMWithdrawals` column family. To have a difference in the time stamp, execute them separately by giving a gap of a few seconds in the same order as given here:

```
INSERT INTO ATMWithdrawals (CustomerId, ActionTime, Amount) VALUES (1,
dateof(now()), 100);
INSERT INTO ATMWithdrawals (CustomerId, ActionTime, Amount) VALUES (1,
dateof(now()), 500);
INSERT INTO ATMWithdrawals (CustomerId, ActionTime, Amount) VALUES (1,
dateof(now()), 50);
```

The following script shows how the physical records are stored in the Cassandra node, and you can see that there is only one row and all the records for the same customer are stored in the same row. The following commands are to be executed in the Cassandra CLI interface:

```
USE PacktCDP5;

list atmwithdrawals;
```

```
Using default limit of 100

Using default cell limit of 100

RowKey: 1

=> (name=2015-07-21 19\:57+0100:, value=, timestamp=1437505078222899)

=> (name=2015-07-21 19\:57+0100:amount, value=4049000000000000,
timestamp=1437505078222899)

=> (name=2015-07-21 19\:53+0100:, value=, timestamp=1437504838401042)

=> (name=2015-07-21 19\:53+0100:amount, value=407f400000000000,
timestamp=1437504838401042)

=> (name=2015-07-21 19\:49+0100:, value=, timestamp=1437504566340301)

=> (name=2015-07-21 19\:49+0100:amount, value=4059000000000000,
timestamp=1437504566340301)


1 Row Returned.
```

The following CQL SELECT command gives an output in a human-readable format. Look at the number of records displayed and see the timestamp. With the descending order of the ActionTime, the recent transactions come first. Note that there is no ordering clause in the CQL statement, but it still displays the records in the descending order of the ActionTime column. This is because of the clustering done when the column family was created.

```
SELECT * FROM ATMWithdrawals;
```

The output obtained is shown here in *Figure 2*:

```
 customerid | actiontime                 | amount
------------+----------------------------+--------
          1 | 2015-07-21 19:57:58+0100   |     50
          1 | 2015-07-21 19:53:58+0100   |    500
          1 | 2015-07-21 19:49:26+0100   |    100
```

Figure 2

Now range queries such as those given in the following commands can be executed to selectively retrieve records for the required purposes. Execute the following command at the cqlsh prompt:

```
SELECT *
FROM ATMWithdrawals
WHERE CustomerId = 1
AND ActionTime >= '2015-07-21 19:50:00'
AND ActionTime < '2015-07-21 19:59:00';
```

The preceding script has to be modified to change the `ActionTime` predicate and have the right timestamp values inserted in the systems where the records are inserted.

Log pattern

An IoT application, or a collection of applications running in an enterprise, generate abundant amount of log entries. Many of the log entries are for the human beings to read, and others are used by other applications. These log entries have all the properties of temporal data. They are processed like temporal data. They are accessed either in the same order or the reverse order of their occurrence. They are used for analytical purposes. They are used for auditing purposes. They are stored for compliance reasons. The processing of a huge amount of temporal data mandates the need to store them just like any other temporal data store. Logs can be collected in Cassandra as a sink. Since application logs have the behavior of temporal data, with the timestamp or timeuuid data types for the Valid Time or Transaction Time, logs can be effectively collected and processed in Cassandra. It is ideal to store all the most commonly needed records in one big row if possible because this will make the process of data access faster. The retrieval pattern must be decided early on during the data modeling stage itself.

Motivations/solutions

Logs living in text files have the biggest problem ever, which is the rollover of the log files. Even though overwriting can be prevented easily, accessing the logs and performing analysis at a later point will be a tedious process as they live in discrete log files. In small applications, it may not be viable or feasible to have a NoSQL data store such as Cassandra to hold the logs. But in an enterprise perspective or in an IoT application perspective, it is more possible. In such cases, there will be a huge number of log writes taking place all the time. Cassandra can take the load as it is designed to support fast reads and fast writes. So, by all means Cassandra is a perfect data store for holding the logs in an enterprise.

Auditing and compliance needs are applicable to application logs as well. In many of the systems, due to these reasons, it is mandatory to keep the logs for a longer period. Whenever such needs are there, the additional constraint is that it has to be stored in the same order as the occurrence of events. Logs fit the bill for temporal data. Proper classification, proper ordering, and preservation are the key things in this use case. Cassandra is designed to store temporal data. As and when the data size increases, if required, more and more nodes can be added to the cluster, providing linear scalability.

A major requirement with respect to logs is that they have to be destroyed after a certain period of time. As part of the compliance and auditing requirements, in many situations it is mandatory to destroy the logs in such a way that they are beyond recovery even from the backups. This brings in two requirements. One is the need to store and process the logs just like any other temporal data, and the other is the ability to destroy them after a stipulated period after generation. Cassandra is a perfect fit for both these needs. Cassandra is a great temporal data storage. With the TTL feature of the records, an end of life for that piece of data can be assigned when inserting data into the data store. Once the TTL time is over, the logs will be destroyed automatically.

The new-generation application logs capture lots of application level internal states, confidential information, performance metrics, and so on. In an application security perspective, it is not safe to leave them in a file system, as this is prone to bringing in security vulnerabilities. Because of these reasons, the information security rules and regulations mandate that the logs have to be moved out of the files stored in file systems. The invariant in this process is that all these logs have to be stored in the same order as they happened. This makes it possible to treat the logs just like any temporal data. Cassandra is a great data store to hold temporal data, and it comes with various data types to hold typed data items. In this case, Cassandra is a great alternative to storing the log entries in system files.

In early-generation applications, authentication and authorization were applicable only to the application and the access to the production data. Because of the hacking threats and many other espionage cases reported in the recent past, the authentication and authorization needs have been extended to the scope of application logs as well. Applications logs are just like transactions in this situation. They have to be treated with all the seriousness and importance provided to transactions strictly by capturing them with the proper timestamp for each and every piece written that shows the behavior of temporal data. Cassandra is a perfect temporal data store, as it supports authentication and authorization.

Because of the proliferation of SaaS applications and the abundance of choice the customers have these days, the SaaS providers are forced to make the service performance metrics as well as many other metrics transparent. Many service providers let the customers access this data. The metrics captured include the application utilization data to application logs. The service providers have to architect the applications in such a way that these are stored in a durable medium that is conducive for easy storage and easy access. All these exposed data items have one attribute tied to them and this is the time at which that data item was valid. In other words, all these data items are temporal in nature. In effect, these data items are to be treated just like any other temporal data in terms of the storage and access perspective. Cassandra is the best industry-strength NoSQL data store conducive for storing temporal data.

Completely unmanned and secure offices are very common these days. The doors and computer systems are operated with access cards or finger-prints. In such establishments, all these access points are equipped with scanners to scan the cards or finger-prints. The applications that take data from these scanners generate a lot of data captured with high-precision timestamps. It is practically impossible to hold these data in ordinary data stores. They have to be stored in highly available clustered data stores without any single point of failure because the security applications are heavily dependent on the availability of the data store. Cassandra is a perfect NoSQL data store with its peer-to-peer deployment model to hold these access logs.

Most of the telecom service providers and Internet service providers generate lots of log-like records with high-precision timestamps capturing real-time service utilization metrics. These are supposed to go to the customers and to many other stakeholders. This falls into the temporal data category, and Cassandra is a great NoSQL data store to hold them and feed them to various applications accessing the data.

Best practices

Just like any other temporal data store column family, even in the case of logs, careful consideration has to be given to analyzing the behavior of the data that is getting into the Cassandra column family, and to see how many records can get into one row. Make sure that it doesn't exceed the capacity of a wide row.

In the case of logs, the timestamp attribute may be applicable to multiple columns. For example, in a log entry, there can be multiple attributes such as type, criticality, component, module, and so on. Here, the timestamp is equally applicable to all the other columns. Because of this, it will be possible to generate multidimensional graphs with time in the X axis. In other words, multiple temporal data sets can be generated from the same record for various analysis purposes. Because of the need to produce multiple temporal data sets, there will be a temptation to create multiple column families for the data sets. This is perfectly fine as long as data integrity is not compromised and errors are not creeping in while splitting the records into multiple column families.

Example

Let's take the example of a mobile phone service provider's application CallLog, where the customer call statistics are logged and captured in this column family. The Cassandra column family CallLog shown in the following screenshot captures these details. The PhoneNumber, YearOfCalls, and ActionTime columns constitute the primary key. The combination of the PhoneNumber, YearOfCalls columns becomes the partition key. The records are stored in the descending order of ActionTime. This is to make sure that the recent call details are accessible first. From a time series perspective, it is a good idea to know how many records there will be per row. For every PhoneNumber and YearOfCalls combination, there will be one row and all the call log records will be in the same wide row. However great the number of calls from the same phone number in a year, it is not going to exceed the capacity of one wide row in Cassandra, which is 2 billion cells per partition.

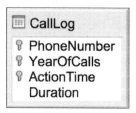

Figure 3

The following script is executed in cqlsh to create the CallLog column family. The assumption is that the key space has already been created:

```
CREATE TABLE CallLog (
   PhoneNumber text,
   YearOfCalls int,
   ActionTime timestamp,
   Duration double,
   PRIMARY KEY ((PhoneNumber, YearOfCalls),ActionTime)
   )WITH CLUSTERING ORDER BY (ActionTime DESC);
```

Now, the column family is created as per the usual practice. The CallLog column family is designed to hold a time series data. The script given below is executed in cqlsh to insert three records into the CallLog column family. To have a difference in the timestamp, execute them separately by giving a gap of few minutes in the same order as follows:

```
INSERT INTO CallLog (PhoneNumber, YearOfCalls, ActionTime, Duration)
VALUES ('+449988776655', 2015, dateof(now()), 10.5);
INSERT INTO CallLog (PhoneNumber, YearOfCalls, ActionTime, Duration)
VALUES ('+449988776655', 2015, dateof(now()), 8);
INSERT INTO CallLog (PhoneNumber, YearOfCalls, ActionTime, Duration)
VALUES ('+449988776655', 2015, dateof(now()), 21);
```

The following script shows how the physical records are stored in the Cassandra node, and you can see that there is only one row and all the records for the same `PhoneNumber` and `YearOfCalls` combination are stored in the same row. The following commands are to be executed in the Cassandra CLI interface:

```
USE PacktCDP5;
list calllog;
Using default limit of 100
Using default cell limit of 100
RowKey: +449988776655:2015
=> (name=2015-07-22 19\:49+0100:, value=, timestamp=1437590998349632)
=> (name=2015-07-22 19\:49+0100:duration, value=4035000000000000,
timestamp=1437590998349632)
=> (name=2015-07-22 19\:38+0100:, value=, timestamp=1437590291915079)
=> (name=2015-07-22 19\:38+0100:duration, value=4020000000000000,
timestamp=1437590291915079)
=> (name=2015-07-22 19\:19+0100:, value=, timestamp=1437589180529548)
=> (name=2015-07-22 19\:19+0100:duration, value=4025000000000000,
timestamp=1437589180529548)


1 Row Returned.
```

The following CQL `SELECT` command gives the output in a human-readable format. Look at the number of records displayed and see the timestamp. With the descending order of the `ActionTime`, the recent log entries come first. Note that there is no ordering clause in the CQL statement, but it still displays the records in the descending order of the `ActionTime` column. This is because of the clustering done when the column family was created:

```
SELECT * FROM CallLog;
```

The output in the human-readable format can be seen in *Figure 4*:

phonenumber	yearofcalls	actiontime	duration
+449988776655	2015	2015-07-22 19:49:58+0100	21
+449988776655	2015	2015-07-22 19:38:11+0100	8
+449988776655	2015	2015-07-22 19:19:40+0100	10.5

Figure 4

Now range queries such as the following can be executed to selectively retrieve records for the required purposes. Execute the following command at the `cqlsh` prompt:

```
SELECT *
FROM CallLog
WHERE PhoneNumber = '+449988776655'
AND  YearOfCalls = 2015
AND ActionTime >= '2015-07-21 19:50:00'
AND ActionTime < '2015-07-22 19:20:00';
```

The preceding script has to be modified to change the `ActionTime` predicate to have the right timestamp values that are inserted in the systems where the records are inserted.

Conversation pattern

Customer relationship management software, popular websites, and many other social networking websites have a chat application as part of the offering. Whenever there is a need to have chat or conversation-related application with the importance of having timestamps for each and every statement in the conversation, it qualifies to be considered as temporal data. These conversations are to be preserved for posterity as a proof of important decisions made. Cassandra with its rich data types and the ability to handle temporal data really well is a perfect NoSQL data store to persist these data points.

Motivations/solutions

Conversations happen all the time between people. Social networking sites are designed to have real-world interactions between human beings. Instead of talking over the phone, the participants here type in the application window whatever they want to say. Here, the important data these individuals are exchanging is text data. Chat between friends and followers in social media is a very common application. Chats take place between individuals, between group of people, and also in a town hall or in a group chat format. Whatever the format, there are individuals and they are having conversation. In software applications, it is important to capture these conversations with the timestamp as their mandatory attribute. Hence, these conversations become temporal. Cassandra is a great NoSQL data store to store temporal data and text data. One of the very first uses of Cassandra was for such a use case.

Some of the new generation social media websites offer conversation between people in the form of pictures and videos. Here instead of the regular conversation by typing text, rich media is being exchanged. Even in this case, the conversational nature of the application remains the same. Each conversation has to be preserved with a timestamp. Effectively, this means the rich media content is exchanged as temporal data. Cassandra is ready to store various types of rich media through its blob data type that can take any arbitrary bytes, and its powerful features to handle temporal data makes it one of the most sought after NoSQL data stores.

Help Desk applications always have interactions with the customers. The customers interact with the Help Desk through various channels related to incidents, service requests, and problems. Whenever a Help Desk ticket is raised to resolve an issue, then a series of business workflows kicks in till the issue is closed. All the steps in the workflow follow the pattern of an orchestrated conversation with timestamps captured at each step. This mandates the need to treat each and every step in the workflow as temporal data. All these different steps are to be stored in a durable medium capable of fast storage, fast retrieval, and search capabilities. Cassandra with other searching and analytical tools is a good option to store these interactions. The need to have a distributed data store to store these conversations is even more important now because many of the Help Desk applications are offered as SaaS delivered through Cloud and hence, the volume of data that is getting ingested is huge. Cassandra is ready to handle the IoT type of data load.

There are many popular messaging applications designed to be used in mobile phones and PDAs. These mobile applications let the device users communicate with other people who use the same service. The communication can happen through text messages, pictures, audio, and video. All these message exchanges have to be stored with the associated timestamp and hence these qualify as temporal data. Some of the popular messaging applications have millions of users and a huge number of conversations taking place every moment. So, a powerful data store is required to store all these types of message exchanges and retrieve them whenever required. Cassandra is a perfect fit for this purpose, and there are a huge number of IoT applications that use Cassandra for such purposes.

Timelines in many social networking sites are a way to organize the contents of an individual user's activities in a chronological or reverse chronological order. To facilitate this, all the user actions are to be stored with proper timestamp as and when they take place. The timeline application reads these actions and their contents and displays them. Here, the temporal data in conversation form is retrieved to be displayed by the social networking application. Cassandra is a great data store to store and retrieve temporal data very effectively.

Microblogging is a recent phenomenon that made the mainstream public participate in the blogging culture. To blog these days, a person need not be a writer. Whatever is coming to a person's mind, whatever raw form it may be in, can be published, and the followers are made based on what is being blogged. Here, the blog entries are short messages supporting rich media content. All these blog entries are stored in the data store with timestamps. They are perfect examples of temporal data. Cassandra is a wonderful NoSQL data store to store these kinds of temporal data.

Online computer games with multiple participants playing at the same time offered in the SaaS model are another good example of conversation-like gaming steps. Each participant takes their turn and makes some moves. All these moves are stored just like a conversation, with timestamps taking the game from one state to the other. These qualify as temporal data when they are stored in the data store in the right order. Many online computer game providers are using Cassandra as their trusted NoSQL data store.

Best practices

Just like any other temporal data store column family, even in the case of conversation-like temporal data, the partition key, the primary key, the clustering columns, and the data types of the temporal data are to be chosen with very careful deliberations. This is to make sure that the right ordering of the data and the number of records coming in a single row are as per the expectations.

Care must be taken while choosing the data types of the temporal data when there is an involvement of rich media content. The applications that are using the data have to be considered along with how those applications require these data, whether they need it in compressed format, raw format, or in an application-specific format, and so on. The latency of the application will be greatly affected if there is a huge amount of pre- and post-processing of the data. Cassandra is open to store many kind of data types, including raw bytes. But it is up to the user to choose a particular data type in line with his/her requirements.

Many social media applications are very secure, and this is also applicable to the data in store. Cassandra security must be studied properly, and it is important to make sure that all the security requirements are satisfied.

Cassandra offers many security features. These include the encryption of data that is in transit, authentication with login and passwords, and authorized access to objects. The **Secured Sockets Layer** (**SSL**) encryption is possible for all the data transmissions between client to node, node to node, and in the CQL shell. As usual, if the Cassandra cluster is being run behind a firewall, then the appropriate set of ports as per the documentation have to be opened up.

Life expectancy of the temporal data must be studied properly during the data modeling stage itself to make sure that unwanted data is pruned after its end of life using Cassandra's TTL feature.

Example

Let's take the example of a help desk application HelpDesk where customer complaints are logged and captured in this column family. The Cassandra column family HelpDesk shown in the following screenshot captures these details. The columns CustomerId, TicketId, ActionTime constitute the primary key. The column CustomerId becomes the partition key. The records are stored in the descending order of TicketId, ActionTime. This is to make sure that the recent action details are accessible first. From a time series perspective, it is a good idea to know how many records there will be per row. For every CustomerId, there will be one row, and all the call log records will be in the same wide row. However great the number of complaints from the same customer, it is not going to exceed the capacity of one wide row in Cassandra, which is 2 billion cells per partition.

Figure 5

The script given below is executed in cqlsh to create the HelpDesk column family. It is assumed that the key space has already been created. One difference in the column family creation is that, for storing ActionTime, the timeuuid data type of Cassandra is used. This is to make sure that there is no collision even if the actions are taking place at the same millisecond value but different nanosecond values:

```
CREATE TABLE HelpDesk (
    CustomerId bigint,
    TicketId bigint,
```

```
ActionTime timeuuid,
Action text,
PRIMARY KEY (CustomerId, TicketId, ActionTime)
)WITH CLUSTERING ORDER BY (TicketId DESC, ActionTime DESC);
```

Now the column family is created as per the usual practice. The HelpDesk column family is designed to hold time series data. The following script is executed in cqlsh to insert three records into the HelpDesk column family. To have a difference in the timestamp, execute them separately by giving a gap of a few minutes in the same order as follows:

```
INSERT INTO HelpDesk (CustomerId, TicketId, ActionTime, Action) VALUES
(1, 10, now(), 'Ticket Opened');
INSERT INTO HelpDesk (CustomerId, TicketId, ActionTime, Action) VALUES
(1, 10, now(), 'Assigned to L3 Support');
INSERT INTO HelpDesk (CustomerId, TicketId, ActionTime, Action) VALUES
(1, 10, now(), 'Ticket Closed');
```

The following script shows how the physical records are stored in the Cassandra node, and you can see that there is only one row for the same CustomerId and all the records for the same CustomerId are stored in the same row. These commands are to be executed in the Cassandra CLI interface:

USE PacktCDP5;

list helpdesk;

Using default limit of 100

Using default cell limit of 100

RowKey: 1

=> (name=10:5f005d00-3167-11e5-b794-e76149b7842c:, value=,
timestamp=1437675574991493)

=> (name=10:5f005d00-3167-11e5-b794-e76149b7842c:action, value=5469636b65
7420436c6f736564, timestamp=1437675574991493)

=> (name=10:a120e160-3166-11e5-b794-e76149b7842c:, value=,
timestamp=1437675256436928)

=> (name=10:a120e160-3166-11e5-b794-e76149b7842c:action, value=4173736967
6e656420746f204c3320537570706f7274, timestamp=1437675256436928)

=> (name=10:7fadf400-3166-11e5-b794-e76149b7842c:, value=,
timestamp=1437675200318814)

=> (name=10:7fadf400-3166-11e5-b794-e76149b7842c:action, value=5469636b65
74204f70656e6564, timestamp=1437675200318814)

1 Row Returned.

The following CQL SELECT command gives the output in a human-readable format. Look at the number of records displayed and see the ActionTime values. Since it is the timeuuid data type, they are not readable for human beings in a sensible manner. But the timeuuid is constructed with a timestamp using the function dateof(), so the timestamp component of a timeuuid column can be extracted, as displayed in the column UUIDTimeComponent in the following screenshot. The timeuuid values are sorted in the order of their timestamp component. The records are displayed in the descending order of TicketId, ActionTime, and the recent action entries, which come first. Note that there is no ordering clause in the CQL statement, but it still displays the records in the descending order of the TicketId, ActionTime columns. This is because of the clustering done when the column family was created:

```
SELECT CustomerId, TicketId, ActionTime, dateof(ActionTime) as
UUIDTimeCompoenent, Action FROM HelpDesk;
```

The output can be seen in *Figure 6*:

customerid	ticketid	actiontime	uuidtimecompoenent	action
1	10	5f005d00-3167-11e5-b794-e76149b7842c	2015-07-23 19:19:34+0100	Ticket Closed
1	10	a120e160-3166-11e5-b794-e76149b7842c	2015-07-23 19:14:16+0100	Assigned to L3 Support
1	10	7fadf400-3166-11e5-b794-e76149b7842c	2015-07-23 19:13:20+0100	Ticket Opened

Figure 6

Now, range queries such as the following can be executed to selectively retrieve records for the required purposes. Execute this command at the cqlsh prompt:

```
SELECT CustomerId, TicketId, ActionTime, dateof(ActionTime) as
UUIDTimeCompoenent, Action
FROM HelpDesk
WHERE CustomerId = 1
AND  TicketId = 10
AND ActionTime >= maxTimeuuid('2015-07-23 19:14:00')
AND ActionTime < minTimeuuid('2015-07-23 19:20:00');
```

The preceding script has to be modified to change the ActionTime predicate to have the right timestamp values that are inserted in the systems where the records are inserted. The functions maxTimeuuid() and minTimeuuid() are used to convert the timestamp strings to the maximum and minimum timeuuid values respectively.

References

- `https://en.wikipedia.org/wiki/Epoch_(reference_date)`
- `https://issues.apache.org/jira/browse/CASSANDRA-7536`
- `http://docs.datastax.com/en/cql/3.1/cql/cql_reference/uuid_type_r.html`
- `https://en.wikipedia.org/wiki/Temporal_database`
- `https://en.wikipedia.org/wiki/Allen%27s_interval_algebra`
- `https://www.facebook.com/notes/facebook-engineering/cassandra-a-structured-storage-system-on-a-p2p-network/24413138919`
- `http://www.datastax.com/2015/02/how-sony-changed-the-world-of-gaming-with-playstation-4-on-cassandra`

Summary

This chapter covered the general nature of temporal data, some specific instances of such data items in real-world applications, and why Cassandra is the best fit as a NoSQL data store to persist temporal data. Temporal data quite often come in different use cases of many applications. Data modeling of temporal data is very important in a Cassandra perspective for optimal storage and fast access to the data. Some common design patterns to model temporal data have been covered in this chapter. By focusing on a few aspects such as the partition key, primary key, clustering column, and the number of records stored into a wide row in Cassandra, very effective and high performing temporal data models can be built.

The 3Vs of big data, namely volume, variety, and velocity, pose another big challenge: the analysis of the data stored in NoSQL data stores such as Cassandra. What are the analytics use cases? How can the distributed data be processed? What are the data transformations that are typically seen in the applications? These will be discussed in next chapter.

6
Analytics Patterns

"Without Big Data analytics, companies are blind and deaf, wandering out onto the Web like deer on a freeway."

– Geoffrey Moore

The ability to process and analyze huge data sets is a real need of the time. Big data is a reality of all organizations as growth of the data that is being generated is enormous. Enterprises are being challenged with the 3Vs of data, described as follows:

- Variety (as in data types)
- Velocity (as in the speed at which data is being generated)
- Volume (as in the amount of data that needs to be processed and stored)

Over the last decade, industry has seen the growth of many data processing and analysis paradigms. When it comes to data processing, it is very difficult to find one tool that does storage of the data, processing of the data, analysis of the data, and presentation of the processed data; but it is always possible to find a set of technologies that work well together to achieve all these requirements.

Persistent data comes in two flavors. One is the data that changes constantly, and the other is data at rest. The latter category is read more often by various applications and is used to process in a journey to discover useful and meaningful information from the data. Data analysis does a lot more than what is described here. The research paper *A Comparative Study of Data Analysis Techniques* gives a very nice description about this as follows:

"Analysis of data is a process of inspecting, cleaning, transforming, and modeling data with the goal of discovering useful information, suggesting conclusions, and supporting decision-making. Data analysis has multiple facets and approaches, encompassing diverse techniques under a variety of names, in different business, science, and social science domains."

Processing big data

To perform data analysis, the first and foremost thing needed is to process the data and transform it for the required analytical needs. In other words, the goal here is to do the analysis, and to achieve this, data processing and data transformation are the means. So, the focus here will be on the data processing and data transformations. The tools and technologies discussed here will revolve around data processing and data transformations. Even though analysis is the end goal, focusing on the data processing and data transformation aspects, the end goal will be achieved.

Over the last decade, many technologies have arrived in the market that process large scale data. These have many things in common. They are open source, they run on commodity hardware, they support clustering inherently, and they are backed by reputed companies to make the technology production-ready at scale.

Apache Bigtop is an Apache Foundation project that helps the infrastructure engineers with tools and a framework for initial deployments, as well as the upgrade of the entire suite of components including Hadoop, Spark, and so on. Here, the focus is on making a set of big data components work together as a solution stack.

Apache Hadoop

Apache Hadoop is one such software library suite that is used for processing huge amounts of data, which is very powerful in batch processing. Originally from Yahoo and now open source, it comes with the common utilities, such as a reliable and distributed file system, namely **Hadoop Distributed File System** (HDFS), a framework for resource and job management, and Hadoop MapReduce, which is a system that does parallel processing of large-scale data sets. But Hadoop MapReduce comes with its baggage of the HDFS, and the data processing is burdened by the read/write cycles from/to the HDFS filesystem. There are many use cases, mainly for performing huge batch processing operations, which Hadoop MapReduce is ideal for. Since the introduction of Hadoop MapReduce, it has become a methodology far and beyond a data processing paradigm. Even though this approach was not new to data processing, huge amount of data to process along with limited computing resources forced companies such as Google to come up with technologies such as Hadoop MapReduce. It is akin to the divide-and-conquer approach to data processing. Compared to many other mainstream open source data processing frameworks, Hadoop MapReduce is an early bird into this space, and is being used heavily even now by companies such as Google, Yahoo, and many others.

Many books and articles use the term MapReduce as an implementation in Hadoop MapReduce rather than as a concept. In other words, they use the term MapReduce to mean Hadoop MapReduce. Map/Reduce is a concept mainly popularized by Google through the research paper *MapReduce: Simplified Data Processing on Large Clusters*. It is a concept and a programming model. Any programming language can be used to do the implementation, and many programming language libraries are available to perform Map/Reduce-like data processing. The only difference is that some of them are really war tested by big companies in their highly scalable infrastructures, and Hadoop MapReduce is one of this kind.

Map/Reduce, as a concept, deals with dividing a big process into a large number of smaller processes, processing them in parallel on a distributed cluster, and finally assembling the results together to produce the final result. It has two phases such as Map phase and then a Reduce phase. The Map phase performs filtering, processing, and sorting. The Reduce phase performs the process of combining the results along with the summarization process. So, typically anybody who wants to do a data processing task will be writing some Mapper functions and Reducer functions in their preferred Map/Reduce library of choice.

In this chapter, wherever there is a need to refer to Mapping and Reducing as concepts, the term Map/Reduce has been used. Wherever there is a need to refer to its implementation from Hadoop, the term Hadoop MapReduce has been used.

Apache Spark

Apache Spark is a comparatively new entrant into the data processing space. It is a general purpose software for large-scale distributed data processing. Spark is an in-memory data processing system that is a lot faster than Hadoop MapReduce. Spark has close integration capabilities with Cassandra, Hadoop, HBase, and Mesos. Most parts of the Spark are written in Scala, and hence it has inherent application development support for Scala.

In this chapter, data analysis examples will be discussed, with Spark as the tool of choice. But considering the tremendous data processing capabilities of Spark, covering Spark in one chapter does not do full justice to it. So, the examples will not include Spark code. The description of the data in Cassandra is given with the column family details, and in some cases, column families used to store the output are also discussed. Pseudocode level details will be given if appropriate where Spark is used to process the data stored in Cassandra. Since the actual code, or exact feature level details of Spark are beyond the scope of this book, a compatible version of Spark that goes well with the examples will also not be mentioned.

Spark has gained a considerable fraction of the market for data processing needs mainly because it comes as a suite of tools. With Spark as the foundation component, tools such as **Spark SQL** to manipulate data using SQL-like queries, **Spark Streaming** to build data streaming applications, **MLlib** as the machine learning library, **SparkR** as a library that R programmers or data scientists can use to run Spark jobs from R shell, and **GraphX** for graph computation can be used as a suite with wonderful interoperability. The other claim from Spark is as follows: "Run programs up to 100x faster than Hadoop MapReduce in memory, or 10x faster on disk;" it is really enticing to anybody who wants to do serious data processing.

Transforming data

Data transformation is a basic need in any data processing paradigm. When enterprises started receiving and accumulating more and more data, the need to have reliable and fast means to do the processing became even more relevant. No data is going to be at rest forever. So, the need to exchange data became another need. Data exchange formats like XML and JSON are some of the most prominent ones in the market these days.

XML revolutionized the data exchange and the corresponding **Extensible Stylesheet Language Transformations** (**XSLT**) revolutionized the data transformation in 1990s. Typically, the data is represented in XML format, XSLT code is used to prescribe the data transformation, and the chosen XSLT processor applies the XSLT on the XML, producing the resulting transformation in the desired format. So, many products came into the market focusing only on the data transformation market.

When the industry started moving away from XML towards JSON, which is becoming the preferred format, lots of technologies came into the market that does the transformation as well that support JSON. JSON4S and JOLT, with the help of very powerful functional programming languages such as Scala, are some of the technologies in the market that serve the JSON transformation space.

When processing and analyzing huge amounts of data in a highly distributed fashion, it is very important to choose a powerful data store, a distributed data processing model such as Map/Reduce, and a data transformation framework in conjunction with a powerful functional programming language.

Spark, with its in-memory data processing capabilities, Cassandra, with its linearly scalable and clustered NoSQL data store that can store huge amount of data, Scala, Java, Python, and R, with its inherent support for parallel operations and concurrency, are a great combination for solutions that can process huge amount of data. There are many other data processing paradigms available in the market, but Spark has been chosen here for the discussions because of its **Domain Specific Language (DSL)** approach to Spark programming and support for multiple programming languages with a uniform programming model across all the supported programming languages.

 Cassandra and Spark have very good interoperability, and the best connector is the Spark Cassandra Connector from DataStax. Spark Cassandra Connector from DataStax is open source as well.

As stated in the beginning of this chapter, Map/Reduce has been around for some time, and many are using it. Here, the first design pattern to be discussed is how some of the existing Map/Reduce programs can be rewritten using Spark, or how to solve Map/Reduce kind of data processing problems using Spark. The second design pattern to be discussed is general data transformations available in Spark.

A brief overview

How can we use Cassandra and Spark together for data analysis? How can we use Map/Reduce-like processing when using Spark? What are the general data transformations that can be performed on the data stored in Cassandra using Spark? This is a very brief overview of these capabilities. All Spark-related discussions are centered around the programming aspects. The clustering, deployments, methods of running jobs, and so on are beyond the scope of this chapter.

The most important data abstraction in Spark is **Resilient Distributed Dataset (RDD)**. For all practical purposes, RDD can be considered as an in-memory table of data coming from its data source. The data source can be text files, files stored in HDFS, Cassandra column families, HBase column families, and so on.

RDD is immutable and hence it is highly reusable and can be cached. Because of the immutability of the RDD, there is an absolute guarantee on the final results because no other process can change its contents once it is created.

Spark comes with a **Read, Evaluate, Print, Loop (REPL)** capable shell. Users can interact with Spark using this shell or write programs in Scala, Java, Python, or R and run as independent jobs.

There are two types of operations that can be performed on a Spark RDD. The first is a set of **Spark Transformations**, and the second is a set of **Spark Actions**. Spark Transformations generally take either a function or other RDD as parameter(s). The function passed as parameter to Spark Transformations define the data transformations on the RDD. For example, assume that there is an RDD containing a set of **key-value pairs** of data **(K,V)**, where Vs are numeric values. If the requirement is to get an RDD containing the (K,V) pairs having only positive V values, in Spark, this is done with one Spark Transformation and one Spark Action. The Spark Transformation filters the data of the (K,V) pairs containing only positive values for V, and the Spark Action collects the filtered (K,V). The result will be a set of (K,V) pairs having only positive values for V.

Spark Transformations without Spark Actions are not meaningful in Spark. Spark Transformations are evaluated in a lazy fashion, meaning that those transformations are carried out only when they are used with a Spark Action. In other words, the transformations are delayed until a point when an action is carried out.

 In this chapter, the focus from Cassandra is slightly deviated on purpose to shed some light onto the analytics platform that is being used along with Cassandra. The important design patterns centered around Cassandra have been already covered in the previous chapters. At the same time, discussions on how Cassandra can be used in conjunction with other data processing frameworks is also equally important. These design patterns are discussed to emphasize the fact that Cassandra is a NoSQL data store that has high interoperability with important data paradigms. So, in all the examples, only the structure of the Cassandra column family will be described.

The Hadoop MapReduce kind of processing can be implemented using a set of Spark Transformations and a set of Spark Actions. The real work is to divide the data processing task to a set of Map and Reduce kind of activities and then pick up the appropriate Spark Transformations and Spark Actions from the Spark programming library to combine them using the necessary data transformation functions written in Scala, Java, Python, or R to complete the task. Depending on the deployment of the data sources and the Spark nodes, the Spark ecosystem will perform the job distribution, parallelization, required computations, and finally collect the results.

In general, data transformations are required to implement business logic in application use cases. Suppose there is a set of key-value pairs in the form (`TimeUUID`, `Amount`) coming from a Cassandra column family. Assume that from these pairs we need to get a set of pairs such as (`Year`, `TotalAmount`). To get the final result, we need to get the year values from the `TimeUUID` values and create the pairs (`Year`, `Amount`). Then, group the pairs that have the same value for `Year`, and from those pairs, calculate the total of the `Amount` values and create (`Year`, `TotalAmount`) pairs, resulting in one pair for each distinct year value. Many of the transformations are performed with the functions written in Scala, Java, Python, or R, and passed to the Spark Transformations and Spark Actions. In functional programming languages such as Scala, functions are first class citizens, and they can be defined and passed around just like any other data types.

Two design patterns will be discussed here, the first is related to Map/Reduce type of data processing. The other is about the general data processing capabilities needed in many of the application use cases. Both are described in the context of Cassandra as the NoSQL data store and Spark as the data processing platform.

Map/Reduce pattern

Whenever there is a need to migrate from Hadoop MapReduce or to develop new Map/Reduce kind of data processing applications, Cassandra can be used in conjunction with Spark and a preferred programming language such as Scala, Java, Python, or R. Divide the data processing task into Mapper and Reducer kind of transformations and actions. Choose the appropriate Spark Transformations and Spark Actions to complete the task.

Motivations/solutions

Many of the day-to-day data processing needs commonly seen in applications can be divided into multiple smaller tasks and executed in parallel. The results can be combined together to produce the final result. A clustered data processing infrastructure in conjunction with a parallel and distributed data processing framework can divide a huge data processing task to smaller tasks and execute them in parallel, thus reducing the processing time considerably. The other advantage of performing data processing this way is that there is no need to invest in highly specialized sets of hardware and software stacks to do heavy duty data processing. The Cassandra and Spark combination is a good choice to do serious data processing tasks in a highly distributed and parallel fashion, especially for real-time or near-real-time data processing needs.

Let's take the example of a retail banking application. From the transaction table, suppose there is a need to find the account level total of all the transactions stored in the table. In this table, there may be one or more transaction records for a given account number. The task is to find the total of all the transactions for a given account number. The same has to be done for all account numbers for which records exist in the table. As a final result, a set of records is to be produced in such a way that there exists one record for each account number having the total transaction amount. This is a task that can be easily divided into smaller tasks, executed in parallel, and finally the results can be combined together. The following list gives an outline of the data processing steps:

1. Create key-value pairs of the form (AccountNo, Amount) by reading the transaction table.

2. The total number of such pairs are distributed to the available processing nodes.

3. In each of the processing node, aggregate the records to have (AccountNo, SubTotalAmount) pairs.

4. Collect all the (AccountNo, SubTotalAmount) pairs from each of the processing nodes.

5. Perform one more round of aggregation on all the (AccountNo, SubTotalAmount) pairs collected from separate processing nodes and produce the final set of pairs in the form (AccountNo, TotalAmount).

In this example, instead of the total of all the transaction amounts, finding the minimum of all the transactions, maximum of all the transactions for a given account number is possible in the same way. But directly finding the average in the preceding method is not possible. For this, it will be necessary to create tuples of the form (`AccountNo`, `CountOfTransactions`, `TotalAmount`) and calculate average out of it. This kind of Map/Reduce data processing tasks can be performed using Cassandra and Spark with the help of the appropriate transformation functions written in Scala, Java, Python, or R.

Top N reports are very commonly used by decision makers. Finding the top 10 account numbers in terms of the total transaction amount, finding the top 10 regions in terms of the total sales amount, and so on are some of the commonly seen examples in applications. In trivial cases where a few thousand records are available, producing these kinds of reports will be pretty straightforward. But when the number of records come in millions and beyond, things have to be handled in a different way. Many such Top N reports can be generated using the Map/Reduce methodology.

For example, continuing with the same retail banking transaction use case described before, we might need to find the top 10 accounts in terms of the total amount of transactions per account number. In the retail banking example, the way to transform key-value pairs of the form (`AccountNo`, `Amount`) to (`AccountNo`, `TotalAmount`) producing one pair for each account number was discussed. Continuing from there, the next task is to find out the top 10 `AccountNo` in terms of `TotalAmount` from the (`AccountNo`, `TotalAmount`) pairs. The following list gives an outline of the data processing steps:

1. Transform the (`AccountNo`, `TotalAmount`) pairs to (`TotalAmount`, `AccountNo`). The reason for performing this transformation is to perform a sort on the key.

2. Sort on `TotalAmount` in descending order in the (`TotalAmount`, `AccountNo`) pairs.

3. Take the 10 records from the sorted list of (`TotalAmount`, `AccountNo`) pairs.

4. Transform the (`TotalAmount`, `AccountNo`) pairs to (`AccountNo`, `TotalAmount`).

Cassandra and Spark, together with some straight forward use of the Spark Transformations and Spark Actions, can be used to generate such Top N reports effortlessly. Unlike the Hadoop MapReduce programs that are really verbose, the Spark programs are very concise and easy to maintain.

Best practices

Whenever a processing task is being modeled as a Map/Reduce kind of form, make sure that the bigger processing tasks can be divided into smaller processing tasks and they all can be executed in parallel, and finally the results can be aggregated.

Spark REPL is a great tool to prototype Spark applications before the actual implementation. Just like any command shell of operating systems, Spark REPL can be used as an interactive shell to try and test the code, before plugging all of them together in a program and run it. This is very useful for seeing the intermediate results, finding the data type of some of the results, and trying and testing whether some of the steps are giving the correct results or not. Right from the import statements of the required libraries, all the programming language constructs can be executed line-by-line in the Spark REPL. Once a set of commands are found to be working as per your expectations, they can be included in the appropriate code package and run as a standalone application.

Whenever a Hadoop MapReduce task is being migrated to Cassandra and Spark, it is not advisable to do a line-by-line porting of the Hadoop MapReduce programs. Conceptualize the whole task and choose the right programming elements from Spark to do this. Use the existing Hadoop MapReduce program just as a pseudocode to develop the Spark applications.

If there are multiple transformations before the results are returned, if possible, do not save the intermediate RDDs. For example, assume that an RDD named DS1 has to go through two transformations (T1 and T2) to produce the final result. Suppose T1 applied on DS1 produces DS2 and T2 applied on DS2 produces DS3. Complete the transformations without saving DS2 before applying T2. If the RDDs contain huge number of data items, the intermediate saves will cause a lot of writes onto the secondary storage, adversely affecting the response time of the application.

Example

Let's take the example of a retail banking application where the Cassandra column family `BankTransactions` captures the account level banking transactions. The column family has the structure as shown in the following screenshot. The columns `AccountNo, ActionTime` constitute the primary key. The `AccountNo` column becomes the partition key. The records are stored in the descending order of the `ActionTime` to make sure that the recent transactions are accessible first. From a storage perspective, it is a good idea to know how many of records are going to be there per row. For every `AccountNo`, there will be one row, and all the transaction records will be in the same wide row.

However big the number of transactions from the same customer is, it is not going to exceed the capacity of one wide row in Cassandra, which is 2 billion cells per partition.

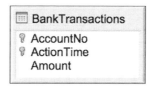

Figure 1

The following script is executed in `cqlsh` to create the key space and `BankTransactions` column family:

```
CREATE KEYSPACE PacktCDP6 WITH replication = {'class':
'SimpleStrategy', 'replication_factor' : 3};
USE PacktCDP6;
CREATE TABLE BankTransactions (
  AccountNo bigint,
  ActionTime timestamp,
  Amount double,
  PRIMARY KEY (AccountNo, ActionTime),
  )WITH CLUSTERING ORDER BY (ActionTime DESC);
```

In this column family, whenever a transaction takes place on a given `AccountNo`, one record gets inserted. The requirement is to find the account level sum of all the transactions in this column family. This is a good candidate to apply the Map/Reduce pattern. The following are the steps required to get the desired result:

1. Read the contents of the `BankTransactions` column family to a Spark RDD.

2. The RDD will have all the column values for any given row.

3. Out of the three columns, only the `AccountNo`, `Amount` columns are required to perform this computation.

4. Apply a map transformation on the RDD to produce another RDD containing (`AccountNo`, `Amount`) pairs.

5. Apply the `reduceByKey` transformation on the pairs (`AccountNo`, `Amount`) to produce the pairs (`AccountNo`, `TotalAmount`) where the function to be passed into the `reduceByKey` transformation produces the sum of the `Amount` column for the given `AccountNo`.

6. Now the transformations are completed, and it is time to use an action to collect the result. The `collect()` action returns another RDD containing the pairs (`AccountNo`, `TotalAmount`). This is save as RDD only if there is a need to do further processing. Otherwise, persist the pairs into secondary storage.

7. If the pairs (`AccountNo`, `TotalAmount`) are to be persisted back to another Cassandra column family, that column family must exist, and the appropriate saving action should be used.

In a traditional Map/Reduce method, the preceding example can be elucidated like this. In this context, the main task is to first find the tasks of the Mapper, and then the Reducer tasks. The complete Cassandra row is to be transformed to key-value pairs (`AccountNo`, `Amount`). This is the Mapper task. The Reducer receives the sorted output from the Mappers from the processing nodes. The Reducer groups the pairs to form something like (`AccountNo`, [`Amount1`, `Amount2`, ...]), producing one pair for each key. Then the desired function is applied to the list, producing the final pairs (`AccountNo`, `TotalAmount`), where the function in this example sums `Amount` the values.

In Spark, all these processing can be performed without writing any complicated Mapper and Reducer programs. It is performed with a few Spark Transformations and Spark Actions, as explained in the preceding example.

Transformation pattern

Data transformation is the heart of data processing, which in turn supports the data analysis. Any framework that is built to perform data processing should have excellent data transformation capabilities in addition to seamless connectivity with various distributed and scalable data stores. These frameworks are built for specific data processing needs of the organizations by themselves, and they consist of a set of commonly available tools used in a specific way to achieve the data processing goals. Cassandra, in conjunction with Spark and a preferred programming language such as Scala, Java, Python, or R, can be used to perform very effective data transformation and data processing. When choosing the programming language, it is better to choose a functional programming language. In functional programming languages, functions are first-class citizens, and they can be used just like any other data type to pass it as parameters to functions and return functions from functions. Scala is ideal in this case because of its functional capabilities to perform data transformation, which are powered by excellent pattern matching features and its highly concurrent collections data structures.

Motivations/solutions

It is impossible to list all the data transformations, that are possible as they are beyond imagination. Most of the time, the business logic dictates the transformations needed. The only thing that is possible is to come up with some of the general transformations that can be used repeatedly in many of the data transformation use cases. Functional programming languages give some constructs that enable the programmers to perform the data transformation easily. Scala's pattern matching capability is a case in point here. When it comes to the data processing frameworks such as Spark, they abstract the commonly used data transformation requirements and offer them as features of the framework. Spark offers two important features related to data transformations, Spark Transformations and Spark Actions.

Mapping a set of data points coming from a data store such as Cassandra from one format to another format is a very common requirement. Consider a set of positive numbers {1, 2, 3, 4, 5, …}. If a square mapping is required on this data set, then the resulting data set should have the positive numbers {1, 4, 9, 25, …}. Here, the transformation acts on all the members of the input data set and produces a new data set using a square function. The square function takes an input x and returns x multiplied by x. Let's represent this function as $x=>x*x$. This can be implemented by creating a Spark RDD by reading data from a Cassandra column family and applying the Spark Transformation `map(function)` by passing the function $x=>x*x$ as the parameter. There is one more Spark Transformation, which works in a similar way to map, named `flatMap(function)`, but it returns a sequence of outputs instead of a single element. Taking a line as input and returning the list of words in that line is a good example of `flatMap(function)` transformation.

Filtering a set of data points coming from a data store such as Cassandra based on a condition to produce a new data set is a very common requirement. Consider a data set of numbers {-2, -1, 1, 2}. If a filtering is required on this data set to produce a data set of only positive numbers, the resulting set should have the numbers {1, 2}. Here, the transformation acts on all the members of the data set and produces a new data set using a filtering function that takes the values one-by-one from the input data set and includes the data items in the resulting set for which the function returns true. Here, the filtering function takes an input x and checks whether x is positive and returns a Boolean. Let's represent this function as $x=>(x>0)$. This can be implemented by creating a Spark RDD by reading data from Cassandra column families and applying the Spark Transformation `filter(function)` by passing the function `x=>(x>0)` as the parameter.

Summarization and aggregation are common transformations. The Spark Transformation reduceByKey(function) is used to perform the aggregation. In the case of a retail banking example, from the pairs of (AccountNo, Amount) representing the individual transactions, if there is a requirement to generate pairs of the form (AccountNo, TotalAmount) producing a single pair for each AccountNo, the Spark Transformation reduceByKey(function) can be used, where the function parameter is the function that performs the summarization.

Similar to the preceding transformations, there are many more available in Spark that can be made use of to perform the required transformations on the data stored in Cassandra column families.

Best practices

Spark provides the transformations but the users have to write the required functions in their programming language of choice. The algorithms used in the functions are completely under the control of the users. A considerable amount of performance testing has to be performed before moving the application to production because some ill-performing algorithms in such functions can completely topple the performance of the whole application, irrespective of using highly powerful data processing frameworks such as Spark.

The advantage of Spark here is that there are rich transformations available in Spark and the users have to write only the required functions that are to be used in conjunction with the transformations, which gives a very uniform Spark programming model irrespective of the user's programming language choice. In the case of Hadoop MapReduce, the coding and testing is much higher and has a lot of dependency on the JVM because of the heavy use of the Java code.

 It is a good idea to unit test the functions separately outside the Spark environment to validate the correctness of the functions.

Spark Transformations and Spark Actions go hand in hand, and it is important to use the correct set from them just as with writing the correct algorithm to solve problems.

Redundant transformations, reverse transformations (such as performing one transformation and, after a few steps, reversing the transformation to go back to the original state without achieving anything from the first transformation) are to be avoided.

Example

Let's take the same example of the same retail banking application used in the Map/Reduce pattern, where the Cassandra column family `BankTransactions` captures the account level banking transactions.

The assumption is that the following script is executed already in `cqlsh` to create the `BankTransactions` column family:

```
CREATE TABLE BankTransactions (
   AccountNo bigint,
   ActionTime timestamp,
   Amount double,
   PRIMARY KEY (AccountNo, ActionTime),
   )WITH CLUSTERING ORDER BY (ActionTime DESC);
```

In this this column family, whenever a transaction takes place on a given `AccountNo`, one record gets inserted. One more assumption to make here is that `Amount` is negative if the transaction is withdrawal, and positive if the transaction is deposit. The requirement is to find the account level sum of only the deposits in this column family. This involves some transformations and following are the steps required to get the required result:

1. Read the contents of the `BankTransactions` column family to a Spark RDD.

2. The RDD will have all the column values for any row.

3. Apply a filter transformation on the RDD by checking whether the `Amount` is positive.

4. Out of the three columns of the filtered RDD, to perform this computation only the `AccountNo`, `Amount` columns are required.

5. Apply map transformation on the filtered RDD to produce another RDD containing (`AccountNo`, `Amount`) pairs.

6. Apply the `reduceByKey` transformation on the pairs (`AccountNo`, `Amount`) to produce the pairs (`AccountNo`, `TotalAmount`), where the function to be passed into the `reduceByKey` transformation computes the sum of the `Amount` column.

7. Now the transformations are completed and it is time to use an action to collect the result. The `collect()` action returns another RDD containing the pairs (`AccountNo`, `TotalAmount`). This save as RDD is performed only if there is a need to perform further processing. Otherwise, persist the pairs into secondary storage.

8. If the pairs (`AccountNo`, `TotalAmount`) are to be persisted back to another Cassandra column family, that column family must exist, and the appropriate saving action is to be used.

References

The following links can be referred for more information:

- `http://www.ijettcs.org/Volume3Issue2/IJETTCS-2014-04-09-077.pdf`
- `http://spark.apache.org/`
- `http://static.googleusercontent.com/media/research.google.com/en//archive/mapreduce-osdi04.pdf`
- `https://github.com/datastax/spark-cassandra-connector`

Summary

This chapter covered several data analysis aspects; it mainly discussed the data transformations. Data transformation is one of the major activity in data processing. Out of the many data processing patterns, Map/Reduce pattern deserves a special mention because it is being used in many batch processing and analysis use cases dealing with big data. Spark has been chosen as the tool of choice to explain the data processing activities. How a Map/Reduce kind of data processing task can be performed using Cassandra and Spark has been discussed, which is very powerful to perform online data analysis. This chapter also covered some of the commonly seen data transformations that are used in the data processing applications.

Many Cassandra design patterns have been covered so far in this book and this chapter concludes the discussions on the design patterns. If the design patterns are not being used in any real-world applications, it has only theoretical value. To give a practical approach to the applicability of these design patterns, an end-to-end application is taken as a case point and described in the next chapter, which is used as a vehicle to explain the applicability of the Cassandra design patterns discussed so far.

7

Designing Applications

"Knowing is not enough; we must apply. Willing is not enough; we must do."

– Johann Wolfgang von Goethe

Learn, assimilate, and apply — it is a continual cyclic process, and this is the mantra. Coming up with design patterns is important but, finding good uses for them is the key. All the previous chapters discussed various design patterns that are very specifically applicable to Cassandra as a NoSQL data store. Applying these design patterns in the right contexts or to the right use cases is very important, and this is going to be the focus of this chapter. In the case of RDBMS, the data modeling has a very strong theoretical support from academia. Moreover, one data model designed for one RDBMS can be easily reused for another RDBMS without any fundamental changes. But in the case of NoSQL data stores, it is different. Each and every NoSQL data store has its own unique way of data modeling. The data modeling techniques in Cassandra are unique to Cassandra, and the same techniques cannot be reused in other NoSQL data stores.

Academia, in collaboration with industry, is defining the standard ways of data modeling for Cassandra. The research paper *A Big Data Modeling Methodology for Apache Cassandra* is a great step in this direction. Before getting into the details of the use cases in which the already discussed design patterns are applicable, a quick glimpse at this research paper would be ideal. This paper gives a good contrast on the ways relational data modeling and Cassandra data modeling are performed. According to this paper, the following steps are taken in relational data modeling:

- Conceptual data model
- Mapping conceptual to relational
- Relational data model

- Normalization
- Normalized relational data model
- Physical optimization
- Relational database schema

According to this paper, the following steps are taken in Cassandra data modeling:

- Application workflow
- Conceptual data model
- Mapping conceptual to logical
- Logical data model
- Physical optimization
- Physical data model

It is a good idea to briefly elucidate the Cassandra data modeling steps given in the preceding list. In Cassandra data modeling, the applications that are going to use the data store come as the first check point, and hence the queries or data manipulation needs from an application perspective are looked at first. In parallel, the conceptual data model is prepared. In the conceptual data model, the entities are identified with their attributes without capturing or looking at the technical details such as data types and things like that. Then their relationships with other entities are also identified. In the conceptual data model, the **entity relationship diagrams** (ERD) are prepared. The logical data model in Cassandra is slightly different from its general theoretical version. It consists of the data model given in the ERD and the query requirements for the application. In other words, for specific queries, there might be a need to introduce redundancy, optimizations, or the creation of additional entities. The final output of these processes is the logical data model. **Chebotko** diagrams can be prepared as explained in the research paper to represent the logical data model. Now, it is time to apply the physical optimizations, such as the identification of the data types, partition key, primary key, and clustering columns, with the required sort order, user-defined data types, and secondary indexes needed. This will be the physical data model from which the Cassandra column families can be created in the appropriate key spaces. In general, the physical data model will have the data store specific details; here, they are Cassandra-specific details.

Before getting into the first Cassandra-based application development efforts, it will be a good idea to have a good read of the research paper *A Big Data Modeling Methodology for Apache Cassandra* to get a good hold on the specifics of Cassandra data modeling. Another excellent book to start with data modeling is *Cassandra Data Modeling and Analysis, C.Y. Kan, Packt Publishing*. Even for veteran data modeling experts, the game is very different in Cassandra. In this chapter, the focus will be more on the use cases of the design patterns discussed so far rather than the data modeling aspects of Cassandra. While describing the data model of the application described in this chapter, only the physical data model will be discussed.

In the previous chapters, individual examples of each design pattern were given. Now, one complete and end-to-end application is discussed here, and the use cases are picked up in such a way that all the design patterns covered in this book will be used. This is to prove the point that these design patterns are fit to be used in many use cases of real-world applications.

A brief overview

An oversimplified version of a fictitious social network application is taken to apply the design patterns discussed in this book. In this application, only some use cases relevant for placing the design patterns have been discussed.

The main application functionality revolves around the users signed-up in this application. Users have connections to other users in the application. Users can post short messages and their connections can like them if they want. The messages cannot be edited or deleted once posted. When a user signs in to the application, the first page displayed is the home page containing message posts from the signed-in user's connections, displayed in reverse chronological order along with his/her own posts. Every user has a personal wall page that displays only the message posts from the signed-in user in reverse chronological order, which is private to the individual user, and with appropriate privacy settings, the connections of the signed-in user can also see the contents of the wall.

The application was originally developed as a fun project and was deployed on the Web, and exposed to the general public. The entire application stack consisted of two physical systems, where one is used for the RDBMS to store the data, and the other is used to serve the web pages. The web server system has an in-memory cache as well to serve the pages of the most frequently visited users. The excellent graphical user interface and the simplicity of the web application caught the attention of the netizens, and the sign-up rate started to grow really fast. The founders started becoming jittery because of the unexpected turn of events caused by the public interest in their fun project. They realized that if the sign-up continued at this rate, the site was going to go down in very short period of time. To bring the situation under control, they disabled the sign-up page of the application and displayed a very courteous message saying that sign-up will be enabled once again after the application was migrated to a better platform with lots of new, exciting features.

Very quickly, the founders, who were developers themselves, included some more people in their core team and started the deliberations to perform their rearchitecture to support the huge scalability needs of the application. They decided to replace their existing RDBMS with Cassandra. As per the plan laid out, the data store rearchitecture was going to be the first priority, and once this was done, the other required application functionality changes were to be taken up later. The rearchitecture was planned in two phases. The first phase would still use the RDBMS for the main use cases, but a Cassandra cluster would also be deployed alongside to store some additional data to improve the performance of some of the web pages and introduce some very high-priority new features. The second phase would replace the RDBMS completely. Once the important changes were completed, the sign-up page would be enabled so that users would be able to create accounts. They also took an intelligent decision that they would not perform a one-to-one porting of the data store from RDBMS to Cassandra. The Cassandra data store would be designed from the ground up, and if required, separate programs would be written to migrate the data from RDBMS to Cassandra. Also, they identified changes needed in the data store connectivity module in the web application. Even though the original development of the application was based on the test-driven development strategy, they decided to improve the automation of their unit tests, integration tests, and the end-to-end use case testing in conjunction with continuous integration. Also, the DevOps team was formed to have development, testing, staging, and production environments promote incremental code changes and realize the value as quickly as possible.

In the preceding example, the application that was used to apply the design patterns involved a lot of business logic, and they were avoided on purpose in order to focus on the data store-related problems, as well as to give emphasis to the Cassandra design patterns that are covered in this book.

Application design and use cases

The RDBMS backend of the application consisted of the core tables given in the following screenshot:

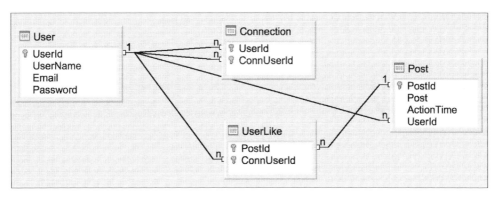

Figure 1

The signed-up user's details are captured in the User table. When a given user establishes a connection with other users, their relationship is captured in the Connection table. When a user posts a message, it is captured in the Post table. When a message is posted, the users from the message owners' connection list can like the message post, and this detail is captured in the UserLike table. The cardinality of the relationships is also captured in the preceding screenshot.

The biggest problem the application faced was in displaying the contents in the home page of the application. The number of users was high, the number of connections each users had was high, and the table joins required to prepare the records was complex. The performance of the home page that contained recent message posts from all the connections of the signed-in users had to be improved. The solution was to design a Cassandra column family PostFeed that contained a denormalized table that contained a new structure which coexisted with the existing RDBMS tables. In this column family, for each of the signed-in user, all the message posts from that user's connections would be inserted. In other words, for a given UserId 1, there were two connections with UserId 2 and 3. When the user with UserId 2 posted a message M1, it got inserted into this column family PostFeed with UserId 1. This was a redundant storage of the data in addition to the original storage requirements. When the user with UserId 1 signed-in, they would see the message M1 on their home page along with the other messages posted by all their connections in reverse chronological order.

The following script creates the required key space and the column family:

```
CREATE KEYSPACE PacktCDP7 WITH replication = {'class':
'SimpleStrategy', 'replication_factor' : 3};
USE PacktCDP7;
CREATE TABLE PostFeed (
   UserId bigint,
   PostId bigint,
   PostedBy text,
   Post text,
   ActionTime timestamp,
   PRIMARY KEY (UserId, ActionTime)) WITH CLUSTERING ORDER BY
(ActionTime DESC);
```

The following table gives a summary of the problem and how it was solved using a design pattern:

Problem solved	Design pattern	Query details
The messages from the connections of a given user stored in the column family PostFeed solved the performance problem of the home page. The home page started getting rendered faster than before.	Denormalization pattern	The single SELECT query with a WHERE condition on the required UserId gave the list of all the messages needed to be displayed on that user's home page. This avoided the need to perform multiple table joins, which improved the response time.

The next priority item of the work was the redesigning of the users' personal wall. It was one single page that contained the signed-in users' message posts arranged in reverse chronological order. Pagination was the only navigation control on this page. Users who had posted lots of messages started to see inflexibility while using the page. A real need was to be able to search the messages by various time ranges. Depending on a given time range, there had to be an ability to retrieve messages posted by the signed-in user. A new timeline widget was introduced on the page. Depending on the selection of the time range on the timeline widget, queries were formed on the fly and started retrieving message posts from the existing table Post of the RDBMS. It started rendering the exact set of messages as per the query. But the biggest issue was performance. Just like creating separate tables for reporting purposes, a new Cassandra column family Wall with the following structure was designed and began to be used as a reporting column family. The column family Wall was designed to retrieve messages posted in any range of time:

```
CREATE TABLE Wall (
   UserId bigint,
   PostId bigint,
```

```
    Post text,
    ActionTime timestamp,
    PRIMARY KEY (UserId, ActionTime)) WITH CLUSTERING ORDER BY
(ActionTime DESC);
```

The following table gives a summary of the problem and how it was solved using a design pattern:

Problem solved	Design pattern	Query details
The messages posted by a given user stored in the column family `Wall` solved the performance problem of the timeline widget on the personal wall of the users. The personal wall's timeline widget started rendering the posted messages faster.	Reporting pattern	The single `SELECT` query with a `WHERE` condition on the required `UserId` and the range queries based on `ActionTime` started rendering the messages needing to be displayed based on the timeline widget's time range selection.

The RDBMS design posed challenges in getting the number of likes for a given message post as well as getting the list of users liking a given message post. The need to display the number of likes for a given message post was important. The need to display the users who liked a given message post was also important. The RDBMS tables don't give this directly and some aggregate queries had to be run whenever a count needed to be displayed on the personal wall page as well as on the home page. Table joins were required to get the list of users who liked a given message post. To serve this need, a new Cassandra column family `LikeCount` was designed with the following structure, and began to be used to store the like count of a given message post as well as the users who liked that message post:

```
CREATE TABLE LikeCount (
    PostId bigint,
    UserId bigint,
    Post text,
    PostedBy text,
    LikedUsers list<text>,
    NoOfLikes bigint,
    PRIMARY KEY (PostId)
);
```

Whenever somebody liked a message post, the above column family `LikeCount` was to be updated with the appropriate details, including the count. This column family stored the list of users who liked a given message post as well, and the Cassandra data type List was used to store this. This served the need to get the list of users who liked a given message post from the same query. The following table gives a summary of the problem and how it was solved using a few design patterns:

Problem solved	Design pattern	Query details
Updating the like count in the column family `LikeCount` solved the need to run aggregate queries every time there was a need to get the count of the number of likes of a given message post. This also solved the problem of performing table joins to get the list of users who liked a given message post.	Aggregation pattern List pattern	The single `SELECT` query with a `WHERE` condition on the required `PostId` started giving the like count of any given message post. The same query gave the list of users who liked a given message post.

Because of the huge performance problems that persisted in the application, many of the important and high-priority requirements were in backlog. Some of the important ones, such as the following, were in the `User` table of the RDBMS:

- Store the password history
- Store multiple e-mail addresses
- Store application preferences

Considering all these requirements and the existing table structure in the RDBMS, it required multiple tables and many joins any time there was a need to extract these data items. The `User` table from RDBMS was migrated to Cassandra. There were strong reasons for doing this. Cassandra has very rich collection data types. All the three requirements listed previously could be achieved with the effective use of Cassandra's collection data types. To serve this need, a new Cassandra column family `User` was designed with the following structure, and it migrated all the data from the corresponding RDBMS table to this column family:

```
CREATE TABLE User (
    UserId bigint,
    UserName text,
    Email text,
    PasswordHash text,
    PasswordHashHistory list<text>,
```

```
    SecondaryEmails set<text>,
    Preferences map<text,text>,
    Connections set<bigint>,
    PRIMARY KEY (UserId)
);
```

The following table gives a summary of the problem and how it was solved using a few design patterns.

Problem solved	Design pattern	Query details
The requirement to have a collection of user attributes without using additional tables was solved by migrating the User table from RDBMS to Cassandra, along with the effective use of the Cassandra collection data types. This also solved the need to maintain the set of connected users in the same column family that were in a separate table of the RDBMS.	List pattern Set pattern Map pattern	The single SELECT query with a WHERE condition on the required UserId started giving all the details of a user without introducing additional tables and without any table joins.

After the success of the User table and the Connection table migration from RDBMS to Cassandra, one more table was migrated to Cassandra. This time it was the Post table. To serve this need, a new Cassandra column family Post was designed with the following structure, and it migrated all the data from the corresponding RDBMS table to this column family:

```
CREATE TABLE Post (
   UserId bigint,
   PostId bigint,
   PostedBy text,
   Post text,
   ActionTime timestamp,
   PRIMARY KEY (UserId, ActionTime)) WITH CLUSTERING ORDER BY
(ActionTime DESC);
```

Even though this column family Post had a very similar structure to the column family PostFeed, that was designed for a different purpose.

Since there was already a column family LikeCount to capture the like details of a given post, the RDBMS table UserLike became completely obsolete. With this changeover, the RDBMS was completely cut off from the application.

The next task selected for application improvement was to give the count of the total number of messages posted by the signed-in user on their personal wall. A new Cassandra column family `PostCount` was designed to capture the count of message posts by a given user. The distributed Counter data type of Cassandra was used to capture the precise counting operation:

```
CREATE TABLE PostCount (
   UserId bigint,
   PostYear int,
   PostCount counter,
   PRIMARY KEY (UserId, PostYear)
) WITH CLUSTERING ORDER BY (PostYear DESC);
```

The following table gives a summary of the problem and how it was solved using a design pattern:

Problem solved	Design pattern	Query details
The new Cassandra column family `PostCount` captured the precise count of the number of messages posted by a given user by making use of Cassandra's Counter data type. This was made possible without using any aggregate query on the message posts whenever there was a need get the total count.	Distributed Counter pattern	The single SELECT query with a WHERE condition on the required UserId started to give the message post count of any given user for a given year.

After all these changes, the application was doing very well, and some of the nonintrusive automated performance tests on the home page started showing some performance degradation. The content of this page was coming from the Cassandra column family `PostFeed`. Additional monitoring was introduced to analyze the root cause of the problem. Along with the test results, close inspection of the column family revealed the fact that whenever a message post was added, that record got inserted many times in this column family based on the number of connections of the user who posted the message. For example, if a given user had 500 connections, one message posted by this user got inserted as 501 records in the PostFeed column family. Along with the existing number of users itself, the number of records in this column family started increasing exponentially. Initial discussions went in the direction of changing the structure of the column family, but that would reintroduce the problem that existed in the RDBMS-backed version of the application. Then it was decided to give a life term for a given record in this column family.

Typically, a message feed page need not keep very old messages. So, it was decided to keep the records in this column family only for 7 days. Cassandra's TTL feature was used while inserting records to control the life of a given message post in the `PostFeed` column family. After 7 days, if a given user wanted to see some of the messages posted by their connections, they could always go back to their connection's personal wall and see the message post. The following table gives a summary of the problem and how it was solved using a design pattern:

Problem solved	Design pattern	Query details
The Cassandra column family `PostFeed` record insertions were performed with the TTL clause in the CQL to make sure that a record inserted into this column family lived only for 7 days. This solved the problem of the exponential growth of the number of records in this column family.	Purge pattern	The single SELECT query with a WHERE condition on the required `UserId` gave the list of all the messages needed to be displayed on that user's home page without any change in the current design. The only difference after this change was that the number of records of this column family had reduced considerably.

The planned rearchitecture, RDBMS migration, and the solution of some of the crucial performance problems were all done, and the application started working as per the expectation. Then the next change in the pipeline was to take a decision on the in-memory cache that was being used in the web application server to speed up the page rendering. Since a lot of performance tuning had already been done, some tests were employed to see the difference in the response times of some of the users' content that was being served through the in-memory cache and some other users' content that was being served directly from the Cassandra column family. The test results showed a difference of only 10 to 30 milliseconds between the response times of these two types of content delivery methods. It was decided that it did not make sense to maintain an in-memory cache just to serve a few users' requests faster, which they were not even going to notice.

The following table gives a summary of the problem and how it was solved using a design pattern:

Problem solved	Design pattern	Query details
The effective use of Cassandra column families and the performance tuning performed reduced the gap between the response times of the content delivered from the in-memory cache and the content delivered from the Cassandra column families directly. This also reduced the need to manage the life cycle of the data residing in the in-memory cache.	Cache to NoSQL pattern	The application layer now needed to read only the data from the Cassandra column families. The complexity of the data access layer API had reduced because the need to maintain the caching layer-related APIs had gone completely.

In this application, most activities took place around the messages posted by various users. The number of users posting messages was huge and it was very important to give high availability to the write operation. In other words, the message post operation had to have less consistency, and hence it would provide high availability. When one message was posted, it went into two column families, Post and PostFeed. Even if there was a slight delay in inserting the messages into the PostFeed, it was acceptable to maintain the consistency. So, the application logic was changed a bit to have a write into the Post column family first with low consistency levels. Once this was completed, an asynchronous business logic kicked in, which read the selected messages from the Post column family with high consistency levels, and inserted into the PostFeed column family with low consistency levels. So, in a Post column family perspective, low consistency writes and high consistency reads for writing on to PostFeed balanced the consistency relation (*(nodes_written + nodes_read) > replication_factor*) briefly notated as *(W + R) > N*. The following table gives a summary of the problem and how it was solved using a design pattern:

Problem solved	Design pattern	Query details
The write into the Post column family was performed with low consistency, providing high availability for the write operation. The read from Post for one use case was performed with high consistency. This solved the problem of the consistency relation balancing.	Write-heavy pattern	No changes to the queries. But the consistency levels had to be set at the driver level — low consistency levels for the write operations and high consistency levels for the read operations.

In this application, user management was another crucial use case. No signed-up user's data was to be lost in any case. So, a high-consistency write was to be imposed when a new user record got inserted into the User column family. But the content of this column family was being read by many other modules of the application, and there the read availability had to be very high. So a high consistency write and a low consistency read balanced the consistency relation $(W + R) > N$. But the challenge was that a high consistency write obviously caused low availability. To work around this problem, a conscious decision of changing the business rule of the sign-up process was made. The following steps give the highlights of the new business rule:

- A new user signs up using the web interface.

- The user data is accepted and passed on to the persistence layer in an asynchronous way.

- A message is displayed on the sign-up response page saying that a confirmation e-mail has been sent to the registered e-mail address.

- The user has to click the link sent in the confirmation e-mail to make sure that the email address is valid.

- By the time the user is done with all these steps, the write operation must have been completed with a very high consistency level. If there is any error because of the high consistency write operation, the user gets another e-mail stating the same and the required work around. This is akin to the commonly seen e-mails sent out when user registration failure takes place or when credit card transaction failure takes place in popular web sites.

- The user is then allowed to sign in once the e-mail confirmation is completed.

After implementing this new business rule of sign-up, the user records were ready to be served for fast reads with low read consistency levels. The following table gives a summary of the problem and how it was solved using a design pattern:

Problem solved	Design pattern	Query details
The write into the User column family was performed with very high consistency providing low availability for the write operation. This was managed by a new business rule. All the read operations from the User column family were performed with high availability and low consistency.	Read-heavy pattern	No changes to the queries. But the consistency levels had to be set at the driver level; high consistency levels for the write operations and low consistency levels for the read operations.

As described previously, the operations in the `Post` column family were to be used in a write-heavy model as well as in a read-heavy model. But these two could not be achieved together while satisfying the *(W + R) > N* consistency relation. So, appropriate business rule tweaks had to be performed to make it a read-and-write-balanced column family. The writes into this column family were done with low consistency. To balance the consistency relation, in one use case a high-consistency read was performed from this column family to make sure that the data integrity was maintained. Note the case of reading from this column family to write onto the `PostFeed` column family described when discussing the write-heavy pattern previously. After this, all the other use cases were using this column family for fast reads. So, in all respects, this column family served as a read-and-write-balanced column family. The following table gives a summary of the problem and how it was solved using a design pattern:

Problem solved	Design pattern	Query details
The write into the `Post` column family was performed with very low consistency providing high availability for the write operation. One use case that was reading from this column family was performed with very high consistency, balancing the consistency equation. In all the other use cases, fast reads were performed from this column family.	Read-write Balanced pattern	No changes to the queries. But the consistency levels had to be set at the driver level. Low consistency levels for the write operations. High consistency level for one read operation and low consistency levels for all the other read operations.

The column family `Post` stored the messages posted by the users in reverse chronological order. At any given point in time, no use case in this application was going to read all the message posts from this column family. The partition key of this column family was `UserId` and the clustering was performed in descending order of `ActionTime`. The common data retrieval pattern was with a filter on the column `UserId` and a range of `ActionTime`. This perfectly fitted the Time Series pattern.

The column family `PostFeed` contained the message posts of connected users including the signed-in user's posts. The partition key of this column family was `UserId` and the clustering was performed in the descending order of `ActionTime`. If a query was given with a filter on the column `UserId` and a range of `ActionTime`, that listed all the messages posted by the signed-in users as well as messages posted by their connections. This listed the messages as if they were in a conversation where the latest message got displayed on top. This perfectly fitted the conversation pattern.

The following table gives a summary of the problem and how it was solved using a design pattern:

Problem solved	Design pattern	Query details
The message posts from the column family Post qualified as general time series data. The message posts from the column family PostFeed qualified as a general time series data as well as following the behavior of a conversation. The time series style data helped many application use cases to retrieve the data from these column families in the selected order without actually spending time and resources to perform the sorting. They were all written and read in sorted order.	Time series pattern Conversation pattern	Both the patterns had one common trait, which was the query predicate which included a range of time.

Service management and use cases

Service management was another crucial organization function that was not formalized so far. Now, Cassandra was deployed in a cluster; application and web servers had their own clusters. The backlog of features to have service supportability and application supportability as well as service management needs were huge, but the top priority was to have a central log containing the following contents:

- Application logs
- Network logs
- Performance metrics
- Audit data
- Monitoring data

All of these were to be classified into different classes such as `<APPLICATION>:INFO`, `<APPLICATION>:WARNING`, `<APPLICATION>:ERROR`, `<NETWORK>:INFO`, `<NETWORK>:WARNING`, `<NETWORK>:ERROR`, `<METRIC>:LOW`, `<METRIC>:25TH`, `<METRIC>:50TH`, `<METRIC>:75TH`, `<METRIC>:90TH`, `<METRIC>:95TH`, `<METRIC>:99TH`, `<METRIC>:99.99TH`, `AUDIT`, `MONITORING`, and so on, and were to be captured in a central log-like data store. Cassandra was doing well and the obvious choice was to use a separate column family to store these logs in a dedicated column family. The column family `Log` was designed to retrieve messages posted in any range of time:

```
CREATE TABLE Log (
  LogClass text,
  DateOfLog text,
  ActionTime timeuuid,
  Message text,
  PRIMARY KEY ((LogClass, DateOfLog), ActionTime)) WITH CLUSTERING
ORDER BY (ActionTime DESC);
```

The partition key of this column family was `LogClass`, `DateOfLog` and the clustering was performed in descending order of `ActionTime`. A composite partition key made sure that in any class of log, the wide row was not exceeding the capacity in terms of the number of records by making sure that for every day, a new row would be created for each class of the log. The following table gives a summary of the problem and how it was solved using a design pattern:

Problem solved	Design pattern	Query details
The records from the column family `Log` qualified as general time series data as well as following the behavior of a central log repository, collecting log data from various sources. The time series data type was easy for various applications to consume the log data for analytical purposes.	Log pattern	The query predicate included the right filter and a range of time.

Since a whole lot of performance optimizations had been completed along with some brand new features such as the timeline on the personal wall, the team enabled sign-up once again and the site was able to grow in terms of the user base. The service management team was actively working with the customers and stakeholders to make sure that uninterrupted service was offered, promoting customer satisfaction. These measures mandated the very close monitoring of the application performance.

The central log that was collecting a whole lot of data needed to be analyzed along with the application data. For this purpose, a new cluster of Cassandra nodes was set up specifically for analytical purposes. The data scientists and the service management teams looked at the data in the analytics cluster to find new pieces of information and patterns. Lots of use cases were proposed for analytical needs and captured in the development backlog. Out of all these, the top priority was for analyzing the application logs specifically for finding the number of application errors and warnings along with other classes of log entries. For this purpose, Spark was chosen, and simple Spark jobs were designed to generate reports with the following requirements:

- Classify the log classes
- For each of the log classes, find the total number of log entries for a given day
- Generate this report immediately after midnight every day

To generate this report, the following transformations and actions had to be performed:

- Extract each row from the column family `Log` for the given day.
- Transform each of the row contents to tuples of the form (`LogClass`, 1).
- Perform a grouping by the key and get the sum of the second elements of the tuple.
- This will generate tuples for each class, having the total number of log entries in that class.
- Collect the final set of tuples and save it in the reporting column family.

The following table gives a summary of the problem and how it is solved using a design pattern:

Problem solved	Design pattern	Query details
Reporting the total number of log entries for each log class was a Map/Reduce type of processing and Spark was used to develop a job for this.	Map/Reduce pattern	Once the Spark job processed the data and filled them in the column families specific to them, then simple CQL queries could be used to retrieve the reports.

Apart from the Map/Reduce kind of data processing needs, many other data processing use cases had been identified. In all these analytical use cases, the most common need was data transformation. The following table gives a summary of the problem and how it is solved using a design pattern:

Problem solved	Design pattern	Query details
Most of the analytical use cases had data transformation needs and Spark Transformations and Spark Actions had been used.	Transformation pattern	Once the Spark job processed the data and filled them in the column families specific to them, then simple CQL queries could be used to generate the reports.

The service management group, equipped with powerful analytical applications, started finding a whole lot of new patterns of information from the data generated. A plethora of new opportunities for this simple but elegant social network application started coming up which redefined the way social network applications were designed, developed, and operated.

References

For further information, the following link can be visited:

* http://www.cs.wayne.edu/andrey/papers/TR-BIGDATA-05-2015-CKL.pdf

Summary

This chapter covered the applicability of the design patterns discussed in this book and used them in a simple but fictitious social network application using Cassandra as the NoSQL data store. The application was originally developed with an RDBMS backend and an in-memory cache. Cassandra was introduced alongside to prove the coexistence of Cassandra with the legacy RDBMS. Then, the RDBMS was completely migrated to Cassandra. Later, many of the existing features of the application were improved by making use of Cassandra's new features to solve the problems effectively and efficiently. Finally, some analytical use cases were also discussed by taking data from the Cassandra column families deployed in an analytical cluster separate from the operational data store.

Index

R

range query 88
RDBMS 1, 2
RDBMS Migration Patterns 29
Read, Evaluate, Print, Loop (REPL) 114
read-heavy pattern
  about 76
  best practices 78
  example 79, 80
  motivations 76-78
  solutions 76-78
Read Repair 68
read-write balanced pattern
  about 81
  best practices 82
  example 83
  motivations 81, 82
  solutions 81, 82
ReportingDatabase
  reference link 25
reporting pattern
  about 11
  best practices 15
  example 16, 17
  motivations 11-15
  solutions 11-15
Resilient Distributed Dataset (RDD) 113

S

Secured Sockets Layer (SSL) 105
service management
  and use cases 139-142
set pattern
  about 36
  best practices 36, 37
  example 37, 38
  motivations 36
  solutions 36
Software as a Service (SaaS) 14, 72
Solid State Disk (SSD) 73
Spark Actions 114
SparkR 112
Spark REPL 118
Spark SQL 112

Spark Streaming 112
Spark Transformations 114
Structured Query Language (SQL) 1

T

temporal data 87, 90
temporal patterns
  overview 91, 92
  references 108
time series 90
Time Series pattern
  about 93
  best practices 94
  example 94-97
  motivations 93
  solutions 93
time-to-live (TTL) 29
timeuuid types 89
transaction 65
transaction time 90
transformation pattern
  about 120
  best practices 122
  example 123
  motivations 121, 122
  solutions 121, 122
Tuple 58
two-phase commit 65

U

Unix Time 88
User Defined Functions (UDF) 91
User-defined Type (UDT) 59

V

valid time 90

W

write-heavy pattern
  about 71
  best practices 73
  example 74, 75
  motivations 71, 72
  solutions 71, 72

Thank you for buying
Cassandra Design Patterns
Second Edition

About Packt Publishing

Packt, pronounced 'packed', published its first book, *Mastering phpMyAdmin for Effective MySQL Management*, in April 2004, and subsequently continued to specialize in publishing highly focused books on specific technologies and solutions.

Our books and publications share the experiences of your fellow IT professionals in adapting and customizing today's systems, applications, and frameworks. Our solution-based books give you the knowledge and power to customize the software and technologies you're using to get the job done. Packt books are more specific and less general than the IT books you have seen in the past. Our unique business model allows us to bring you more focused information, giving you more of what you need to know, and less of what you don't.

Packt is a modern yet unique publishing company that focuses on producing quality, cutting-edge books for communities of developers, administrators, and newbies alike. For more information, please visit our website at www.packtpub.com.

About Packt Open Source

In 2010, Packt launched two new brands, Packt Open Source and Packt Enterprise, in order to continue its focus on specialization. This book is part of the Packt Open Source brand, home to books published on software built around open source licenses, and offering information to anybody from advanced developers to budding web designers. The Open Source brand also runs Packt's Open Source Royalty Scheme, by which Packt gives a royalty to each open source project about whose software a book is sold.

Writing for Packt

We welcome all inquiries from people who are interested in authoring. Book proposals should be sent to author@packtpub.com. If your book idea is still at an early stage and you would like to discuss it first before writing a formal book proposal, then please contact us; one of our commissioning editors will get in touch with you.

We're not just looking for published authors; if you have strong technical skills but no writing experience, our experienced editors can help you develop a writing career, or simply get some additional reward for your expertise.

Real-time Analytics with Storm and Cassandra

ISBN: 978-1-78439-549-0   Paperback: 220 pages

Solve real-time analytics problems effectively using Storm and Cassandra

1. Create your own data processing topology and implement it in various real-time scenarios using Storm and Cassandra.

2. Build highly available and linearly scalable applications using Storm and Cassandra that will process voluminous data at lightning speed.

3. A pragmatic and example-oriented guide to implement various applications built with Storm and Cassandra.

Mastering Apache Cassandra
Second Edition

ISBN: 978-1-78439-261-1   Paperback: 350 pages

Build, manage, and configure high-performing, reliable NoSQL database for your application with Cassandra

1. Develop applications for modeling data with Cassandra 2.

2. Manage large amounts of structured, semi-structured, and unstructured data with Cassandra.

3. Explore a wide-range of Cassandra components and how they interact to create a robust, distributed system.

Please check **www.PacktPub.com** for information on our titles

Learning Apache Cassandra

ISBN: 978-1-78398-920-1   Paperback: 246 pages

Build an efficient, scalable, fault-tolerant, and highly available data layer into your application using Cassandra

1. Learn to install and use Cassandra from the ground up.

2. Design rich schemas that capture the relationships between different data types using compound primary keys.

3. Master the advanced features available in Cassandra 2.0 through a step-by-step tutorial that builds a real-world application's database layer.

Cassandra High Availability

ISBN: 978-1-78398-912-6   Paperback: 186 pages

Harness the power of Apache Cassandra to build scalable, fault-tolerant, and readily available applications

1. Master the essentials behind building highly available applications on top of Apache Cassandra.

2. Learn how to effectively configure and deploy Apache Cassandra across multiple data centers.

3. Avoid common pitfalls that prevent applications from achieving 100 percent uptime.

Please check **www.PacktPub.com** for information on our titles

Printed in Great Britain
by Amazon